# WRITING LOCAL HISTORY
## A Practical Guide

also published by the Bedford Square Press:

*Armorial Bearings of the Sovereigns of England*
*Building Stones of England and Wales*
*The Civil War and Interregnum: sources for local historians*
*Hedges and Local History*
*How to Read a Coat of Arms*
*Landscapes and Documents*
*Local History and Folklore*
*Local Taxation: national statutes and the local community*
*Maps for the Local Historian: a guide to the British sources*
*The Rural Constabulary Act 1839: national statutes and the local community*
*Tithes and the Tithe Commutation Act 1836: national statutes and the local community*

# Writing
# Local History
## A Practical Guide

**David Dymond**

Published for the
BRITISH ASSOCIATION FOR LOCAL HISTORY
by the
BEDFORD SQUARE PRESS | NCVO

Published by the
BEDFORD SQUARE PRESS of the
National Council for Voluntary Organisations
26 Bedford Square London WC1B 3HU

ISBN 0 7199 1048 X

First published 1981
Reprinted with corrections 1982

Printed in England by Lamport Gilbert Printers Ltd., Reading

To the local historians with whom I have worked
at Madingley Hall and Flatford Mill

'But a new intensity of investigation has forced the narrowing of the geographical and spatial horizon. As we shall see, instead of the majestic sweep through hundreds of years of European history, we are confined often to one English county, or even one village.'

Alan Macfarlane, Witchcraft in Tudor and Stuart England (1970), p. 5

'Eventually indeed, when the history of English towns and villages has been written as it ought to be, the study of English history itself will also be revolutionised.'

Alan Everitt, Ways and means in local history (1971), p. 5

'I have confessed to you that I am fond of local histories. It is the general execution of them that I condemn, and that I call *the worst kind of reading*. I cannot comprehend but they might be performed with taste.'

Letter from Horace Walpole to the Rev William Cole, 13 March 1780

# CONTENTS

Foreword                                                    ix
1  The state of local history                               1
2  Finding a subject                                        4
   Place                                     5
   Time                                      7
   Theme                                     9
   Group-work                               11
   Aids to research and teaching            12

3  The search for sources                                  14
   The storage of information               14
   The use of printed sources               15
   The gaining of background knowledge       16
   Making human contacts                    17
   Physical evidence                        18

4  Transcribing and translating                           19
   A note on dating                         21

5  Analysis and synthesis                                  22
   Methods of analysis                      24
   Relating varied sources                  27

6  The end product                                         30
   Preliminary notes and the first draft    32
   Some guidelines for writing              34
   Producing a final draft                  37
   References                               42
   Appendices                               43
   A final reminder                         43
   Further reading                          44

References                                                 45

Appendices                                                 49
   1  Published works                       49
      *Transcripts and translations*
      *Indexes to original sources*
      *Bibliographies of secondary works*

*cont.*

2 Basic rules for transcribing documents 51
   *Palaeography: a reading list*
3 Historical dating 53
4 Analysis 54
5 The historian and his sources 60
6 The organisation of a piece of historical writing 63
7 Examples of writing, with detailed critique 71
8 Short extracts of written history 76
9 An exercise in historical writing 79
   *A suggested draft* 81
10 The characteristics of historical language 82
11 Styles of historical writing 83
12 Some rules recommended for setting out references 88

**Index** 91

# FOREWORD

For ten years or more I have been waiting for someone else to write this book but my patience is finally exhausted. Although a number of distinguished historians – such as W. G. Hoskins, W. B. Stephens, R. B. Pugh and Alan Rogers – have written important books about local history, they have been primarily, if not exclusively, concerned with evidence (that is to say, the manuscripts, printed works and physical remains which are the raw materials of the subject).[1] This already considerable literature will no doubt continue to grow as new sources are found and 'developed' but, apart from H. P. R. Finberg's witty essay on 'How not to write local history', we have nothing which discusses in any detail how work on sources is converted in the mind, and through the pen, of the local historian into a personal reconstruction of the past.[2]

Yet the need is abundantly clear. As they contemplate the challenge of writing, individuals and groups no longer suffer in silence but are asking for clear guidance. Unfortunately, all they are normally given is more talk about palaeography and sources. My intention therefore in writing this book is to help correct what I see as a dangerous imbalance, and to assist those local historians who are determined to make their own contribution to knowledge in a written form.

The actual and potential writers of local history now include a wide range of ages, interests and backgrounds: apart from professional historians, we have teachers, journalists, members of national and local societies, adult classes, individuals fascinated by the history of their own towns and villages, postgraduate and undergraduate students, and pupils in schools. Furthermore, local history is now written by outside specialists such as sociologists, anthropologists, planners, geographers, biologists, students of literature and others; by importing their own methods and concepts, they are enriching a subject which is already recognised as a fundamental and inexhaustible quarry of human experience.[3] Now there is talk of 'giving history back to the people'.[4] Ordinary citizens are encouraged to contribute their own evidence, oral and documentary, and to compile their own accounts of life in the past – whatever their educational standards and levels of literacy. The Centerprise booklets from the East End of London have already shown some of the exciting possibilities.[5] In these ways, the study and writing of local history can give much more than personal satisfaction: it may actually break down social and educational barriers, give the lives of older people a new relevance, and help to make local democracy more informed and sensitive.

I believe that the scope and appeal of local history will continue to widen, and that the personal and social relevance of the subject will be increasingly recognised, but only if we learn to communicate better and in particular improve our use of the written word.

## The arrangement of the book

In spite of the danger of over-simplification, the text has been deliberately subdivided into six sections, so that the reader can easily find what interests him most.

The twelve appendices provide more detailed information, practical exercises and examples of writing. Originally produced as teaching aids, I hope they will have value for individuals and groups, and provide teachers with ideas which are worth adapting to their own circumstances.

## Acknowledgements

I am grateful for the encouragement I have received, in writing this book, from the Executive Committee of the Standing Conference for Local History, and from its publications sub-committee. The following individuals are not responsible for any of the views expressed, but have helped me greatly with their comments and criticisms: Robin Chaplin, John Higgs, John Marshall, Bettie Miller, Lionel Munby, Jack Ravensdale, Alan Rogers and Joan Thirsk. My deepest gratitude, however, is reserved to the numerous local historians whom I have met over the years in extra-mural classes, residential courses, local societies and county committees. It is they who have shown me that local history is much more than an academic subject and that its real potential, both for individuals and for society, has yet to be realised.

# 1. THE STATE OF LOCAL HISTORY

Although local history has developed remarkably in the last thirty years, all is not well with the subject. In spite of the foundation of numerous societies, a spate of publishing and the increasing provision of courses and qualifications, one still meets many people who yearn to make a contribution but do not know how. The educational development of the subject, which was confidently predicted in the 1950s and '60s, has turned out to be very uneven in coverage, and to have terrifyingly variable standards. Even the sudden burst of new educational schemes in the last few years has had as much to do with personal empire-building and the survival of shaky institutions as with the subject itself. The fact cannot be denied that local history is seriously fractured and divided. Differences of approach are sometimes discussed, rather superficially, as pairs of opposites: the academic and popular, professional and amateur, regionalist and parochialist, those concerned mainly with primary sources and those with secondary, those based on wide chronologies and those based on narrow, and so on. Of course, variety in one important sense invigorates the subject, and in practice such groups frequently overlap. However, local historians still have a dangerous tendency to ignore each other, to publish and proselytize with blithe independence, and to show little interest in discussing objectives, standards and co-operation. As a consequence, much local research is not as comparative and cumulative as it should be, and effort is wasted. Clearly, our best hope for the future lies in improving the channels of communication between local historians of all kinds. It is widely recognised that we need better organisation at a national level, but we need it even more in individual counties or regions.

In this pattern of rich but confused diversity, I would like to focus on one aspect which is at least tangible: the way local history is interpreted and written. More often than not, it seems to me, good standards of research and writing do not go together. On the one hand, experienced practitioners of local history are often unwilling or unable to communicate their findings with sufficient clarity (though admittedly this is now common to many academic subjects); on the other hand, much dedicated and loving work is published with standards of research which are not rigorous enough.

The paradox can be illustrated by two short examples. The first was written by a university teacher. He is discussing an important problem which is familiar to most practising historians, the difficulty of using two or more documents which *may* be referring to the same historical individual:

> 'From this claim, if it stands, it follows that historical existence claims, historical predicate corroboration and the growth of

historical knowledge in general, presuppose historical record linkage.'

One can perhaps understand how an educated man may produce such an obscure sentence in a preliminary draft, but how can he in good conscience submit it for publication, and how finally can it be accepted by an editor and publisher, as this was? Writing of this kind surely indicates that something is wrong not only with our standards of general education, but also with the specific way in which we train academics to do research.[6]

The second example is utterly different in flavour, and was written by an interested and industrious person who wanted to contribute to the history of her own village:

'It seemed such a pity to have all these bits and pieces lying about, so I decided to put them in chronological order.'

This sad apology reminds us of the plight of many would-be local historians. The growing popularity of the subject means that an increasing number of people amass information but unfortunately make no creative use of it. Some of them (certainly not all) have genuine critical and literary ability, but have never been sufficiently helped to face the challenge of evidence, or to write. It is now easier than ever to be buried by the information which one finds.

Many writers of local history are therefore torn between two false ideals: academic incomprehensibility and undemanding readability. Generally professionals commit the first fault and non-professionals the second, but not invariably so. The situation is made worse by those publishers who either abuse the popular appeal of the subject by commissioning inadequate books from ill-prepared authors, or allow poorly written academic work to pass. Editors of some journals must also accept a similar measure of blame. In every English county we now see the frequent publication of badly prepared and badly written history, which in turn makes it more difficult for others to teach the subject adequately.

In addition, growing numbers of students in schools, colleges and universities are required to do projects and dissertations based on original evidence. Little of this work is published, but it is an increasingly important kind of historical and educational experience. While some of these young people are excellently supervised and derive considerable benefit from the exercise, a frighteningly high proportion are allowed to choose unsuitable topics, get little or no guidance in their work, are not provided with sufficient bibliographical aids, have great difficulty in interpreting their sources (if they find them), and in the end write joyless prose which, tragically, may not truly reflect their abilities.[7] Geoffrey Elton is right to warn us that 'documents thrown naked before the untrained mind turn from pearls to paste'.[8] Unfortunately, a considerable number of educational projects show that both students *and* teachers are unprepared for this kind of work. The final problem is to guarantee a fair system of assessment. When the examiner is not familiar with the secondary sources which a student has used, he cannot always be sure whose thoughts and style he is actually reading.

But does this range of written standards matter greatly, when fine works of local history are published quite often? My answer is that it does matter, for a variety of reasons. First, highly variable standards of writing condemn local history in the eyes of too many people. This is one reason why, for example, hundreds of teachers and students dismiss local history as amateur, antiquarian and 'parochial'. Secondly, I do not believe that our present standards are inevitable for all time and can never be raised. Local history need not be written obscurely or uncritically – especially if the right kinds of help and teaching are provided in the future. The third and last reason is the most important. Because local history is about ordinary people and everyday life, and therefore has an important educational and social role to play, we who profess the subject should value clear, stimulating writing particularly highly.

Indeed ours is a very special subject which interests more people than any other branch of history, and gives rise to a specially voluminous and varied literature which librarians and booksellers, in their embarrassment, usually classify as 'English topography'.[9] No other subject in the academic spectrum can so easily bridge the gulf between the specialist and man-in-the-street. In fact it frequently annihilates that gulf because the 'expert' turns out to have had no special training, and the 'amateur' is often able to contribute special skills and knowledge of his own. Could anything be more socially beneficial in this age of excessive specialisation, qualification-mongering and professional touchiness?

For all its undoubted imperfections, I hope that this book will be of some help to those who, particularly for the first time, find themselves tempted, or required, to write local history. Of course it runs the risk of criticism from all sides: it will say things which to the part-time historian seem pedantic and supercilious, and other things which to the established or professional writer are self-evident or impertinent. However, my main purpose is simply to focus attention on our standards of research and writing, in the belief that this is one way to expand our command and enjoyment of the subject. May it be judged in this light.

# 2. FINDING A SUBJECT

One of the most important problems which the local historian should face is so elementary that it is often overlooked: he must carefully define a subject for research, and be prepared to re-define it as his work proceeds. With a clear objective, however large or small, he can concentrate attention more effectively and recognise the potentialities and relevance of evidence as it is found. Otherwise it is easy to waste time, not infrequently a lifetime, vaguely enjoying the collection of many disparate 'facts' but not thinking about their relative value in a defined project.

Our choice of subject is influenced by a host of factors, personal and historical: our existing knowledge, our educational and family background, the aspects of life which interest us most, the number of people working on the project (group-work is becoming ever more popular, especially in adult classes and local societies), and of course the availability of sources. Frequently subjects have to be re-defined or at least modified, as new evidence becomes known. Some topics lead to the discovery of abundant sources, in which case the terms of reference may have to be reduced; conversely other topics reveal an embarrassing lack of evidence, and therefore the coverage may have to be widened. But these are not invariable rules. A small group of documents can be used, with ingenuity, to tell a fascinating human story.

The main stimulus in choosing a subject is *not* a full appreciation of the relevant sources. We cannot possibly know all the evidence before we start, though we hope to know some of it. *The unavoidable starting-point must be a deep and genuine interest in some aspect of human life which we believe is significant.* This means that we must be prepared to probe our own motives with care. We must ask ourselves why we are attracted to a particular slice of history. Is it because it seems romantic or quaint, or because an interesting document or building suddenly took our fancy? Is there a danger that our fascination with bits of evidence will divert us from the main task of writing about people? Of course, to tell any kind of human story we must have sources, usually a collection of documents, and the discovery of a cache of documents has frequently led to a distinguished work of history. But evidence is there to be used, processed and therefore transformed into original, humane history.

In practice our interest often focuses on a subject which nobody has tackled before. Even so, there are always points of contact with what other historians have already written. In that sense, no piece of research is ever divorced from existing knowledge. Woe betide the historian who forgets this, and writes as if he were in a vacuum. Looked at more realistically, therefore, our wish may be to fill certain gaps in the record, or to show our dissatisfaction with the existing state of knowledge, and thus to contribute to a current debate or controversy. At any rate, on narrowing down the options, we soon find that three dimensions have to be adjusted: subject, place and time. In order to satisfy ourselves and our evidence we must decide, sooner or later, on a particular theme of human history, in a particular area, over a particular length of time. Of course the number of variations open to us is almost infinite. This is why local history shades into other forms of history, and why we should never waste time arguing that local history is a separate, independent discipline. At best it is merely an emphasis within the broad spectrum of historical studies.

## Place

For generations the majority of local historians have chosen to work on the town or parish in which they live. This is not surprising because one's home district is part of one's life: its houses, its hidden corners, the church or chapel which stands for something more than the earth-bound, sad but evocative tombstones, the fields and their names, the river or canal which was so attractive in childhood, the offices and factories which symbolise work and routine – all these represent the lives of countless people who lived, worked and died there. The place itself is primary evidence, as much as the documents we hope to find, and for many of us was the original spur to our historical imaginations. Therefore, a considerable number of us prefer to write about the places we know and perhaps love. Whether or not we can do justice to the undertaking is another matter.

Another equally good reason for studying a particular place can be that it is well-documented, either in a general sense or by having a single outstanding source. David Hey wrote his fascinating account of Myddle in Shropshire, not because he lived there, but because it offered one of the most remarkable sources known to English historians – a contemporary account of its inhabitants by a seventeenth-century resident, called Richard Gough.[10] Sadly, many local historians miss good opportunities because they are not willing to sample larger areas. Parishes within, say, a deanery or hundred will show massive variations in the quantity and quality of their records, but a few outstandingly good sources will always cry out for attention. Similarly each individual parish will have its own strengths and weaknesses which have to be recognised and allowed for. In my own corner of Suffolk, within four contiguous parishes, Stanton has an unusually rich collection of medieval charters, Walsham-le-Willows has outstanding manorial surveys and good poor-law records, Bardwell has the accounts of a late medieval gild and a good town-book, and Stowlangtoft has the autobiography and correspondence of a seventeenth-century squire who was also a national figure. Simply to investigate the life of a single parish, one would have to look at the resources of the whole district. Although the local historian rightly stresses the traditional significance of parish boundaries, in an age when they are largely overlooked, he must not allow them to limit his own vision. Of course, Richard Gough's description of Myddle is quite exceptional; in general we are looking for sources which are relevant to a chosen topic, and are sufficiently organised in their layout to allow proper analysis.

In recent years, a small number of professional historians have chosen to study *groups* of communities. Thus Margaret Spufford in her *Contrasting communities* worked on three widely-spaced Cambridgeshire parishes which she saw as representative of different sub-regions within the county. Her book almost coincided in publication with Jack Ravensdale's *Liable to floods* which also dealt with three Cambridgeshire parishes, but this time adjacent ones at the southern end of the Fens.[11] Their approach, which Alan Rogers has usefully dubbed 'comparative local history', was pioneered in the 1950s by writers like David Chambers and is being accepted by a growing band of historians.[12] By the device of comparison they are able to bring into sharper focus both the common inheritance and real uniqueness of individual communities – two major objectives in local research.

At a higher level of generalisation, a few writers have chosen to study larger groups of parishes, in the shape of hundreds, wapentakes and deaneries. A good example is H. E. Hallam's *The new lands of Elloe* which dealt with the early reclamation of fenland and marsh in a corner of Lincolnshire. This approach is not as common as might be expected, but it could be one of the growth-points of the future. More often the chosen unit of study is a recognisable geographical area, for example, the Weald of Kent or a Yorkshire dale;[13] or it is a complete county. This last genre of historical writing has an antiquity which stretches back to the sixteenth century, to such names as William Lambarde and Richard Carew, and is still very much alive today. County histories of various kinds, containing many different blends of information, are still regularly published. Furthermore, several groups of specialists frequently decide to work on this scale. For example, historians interested in local government and politics have chosen the county because it is an obvious and significant unit of administration.[14] Other groups such as topographical and agricultural historians often make the same choice, but for less obvious reasons: they may be swayed more by archival than historical considerations.[15]

Finally we must not forget the growing interest in whole regions. These are large groups of communities which may have had, at particular periods of the past, certain common characteristics, a similar blend of social and economic interests. Put simply, they are communities of communities. As more documents and local histories are published, and as more people are trained in economic and social history, so this synoptic approach tempts a growing number of teachers and writers. Studies have been made, for example, of the agrarian economies of South-west Wales and the Forest of Arden; of the industrialisation of the West Midlands, the North-east and the Medway Valley; of the spread of particular industries, like the making of footwear in the East Midlands; and of scattered communities which nevertheless share important features, such as ports or holiday resorts with their seasonal occupations.[16] Geographical scale is really an irrelevance to the concept of a region: it may be as small as Merseyside or as large as the Scottish Highlands.

Professional historians are now busily debating regional history. Is it distinguishable from local history? What indeed is a region? To some extent this debate is artificial, for local history has always had a regional dimension, or should have had. To teach local history without discussing the wider patterns offered by administrative districts, by geographical regions, by economic relationships and by the nation itself, is to trivialise and disorientate the subject. In fact this debate largely arises from the difficulties of teaching local history at an undergraduate level: that is, teaching the values and priorities of local history to people who are not interested in the same individual places, and incidentally doing it in a way which earns the respect of other kinds of historian.

Any local or regional study which does not convey a clear sense of place is stunted. A recently-published study of an Essex village gives fascinating insight into the increasing polarisation of rural society in the seventeenth century, but reads as if the writers had never visited the place. A map of 1597 was not reproduced, and the topography of the traditional village and farming landscape, which are extraordinarily well preserved, was barely mentioned.[17] The physical setting is one of the major factors which make each community unique, as well as being important historical evidence in itself. Although those who specialise in political, economic and social history often overlook the importance of place, the local historian can never afford to do so: by a combination of words, maps and illustrations he must give the reader a coherent impression of the landscape or townscape which contained his human story.

# Time

The traditional kind of parish history normally employs a very broad chronological canvas. It usually brings the story down to the present day, or at least to the nineteenth century, but the starting point varies greatly. It may be the familiar years of 1066 and 1086 or, as in the case of Hoskins'

7

*Midland peasant,* the Anglo-Saxon conquest, or even the scattered but intriguing relics of prehistory. This kind of 'general' history has always been difficult to write and now, because of the staggering proliferation of sources and techniques, it is even more difficult. Nevertheless many writers are still tempted to cover local history from A to Z and some, it must be admitted, score notable successes.[18]

A parish or town history need not always be a fat tome like Sir Matthew Nathan's *Annals of West Coker* with its 521 pages; it may be a relatively slim volume or simply a pamphlet.[19] In one sense, the shorter the treatment, the greater the selectivity and judgement which the local historian has to exercise. He is forced to identify the most significant issues in the history of his community. For example, an author commenting recently on a Fen-Breckland parish had the courage to say that the three main events in its history were the drainage of the fen in the seventeenth century, parliamentary enclosure in the early nineteenth, and the rapid expansion and suburbanisation of the last generation.[20] Whether or not he is right, this is the kind of judgement and debate which local history should contain. Incidentally, it would be helpful if every local historical society set about the task of discussing, and attempting to identify, the outstanding themes of its area's history, but only rarely does this happen.

Because of the increasing sophistication of research and the sheer number of sources now available, many local historians are working within much narrower chronological limits. Thus David Hey in his study of Myddle was primarily concerned with the sixteenth and seventeenth centuries, and David Jenkins limited his work on South Wales to merely 'the turn of the twentieth century'.[21] Many part-time historians would undoubtedly contribute more to knowledge and keep in better touch with specialists if they attempted a less ambitious and more manageable chronology. For example, an immense amount of research needs to be done on the nineteenth century, yet the period is frequently neglected by local enthusiasts – even though its sources are comparatively abundant and might present the best opportunities for creative work.

Finally, while on the subject of time, let us remember the value of recording the present for local historians of the future. Even though the twentieth century produces vast quantities of paper, film and tape, many aspects of local life will have no record *unless we make it now.* Most discussions are not minuted; many decisions are made on the telephone; most local events are not recorded at all. Because of our close involvement, we cannot create a full and balanced picture of our own times, but at least we can greatly amplify the evidence to be left behind. Thus some county organisations encourage local people to make notes, build up scrap-books and take photographs. Similarly, it is entirely appropriate that one of

Britain's best-known local historians is keeping a 'black book' on the contemporary political history of his town, which he will bequeath to the local archives: he wants to make a contribution to truth and, as he says, time is on his side. This approach is of great personal benefit: from the contemporary world of which we form part, we as historians derive not only our curiosity about the human condition, but also our awareness of how evidence is lost and truth is clouded.

## Theme

Just as the trend today is towards the study of shorter periods, so proportionally fewer people are attempting to embrace all aspects of local life, and therefore all kinds of evidence. They are increasingly likely to choose a major or central theme which specially interests them, be it agriculture, industry, population, nonconformity, the poor-law or one of at least a dozen others. The sources behind any of these themes may be quite sufficient to sustain a satisfying piece of work. Furthermore, many of these subjects have now become specialisations in their own right, with their own professional experts, societies, textbooks and journals. Nowadays professionals are not normally content to call themselves simply 'historians' but claim to be members of some sub-species: economic, social, agricultural, educational, business, labour, ecclesiastical, medical, oral, medieval, early modern, and so on. Key figures in the world of local history also wear other hats, and call themselves economic historians, or urban historians or whatever. Now part-timers are tending to follow suit, because they too want to tackle something which is manageable. After all, some of the best and most active students of local history are those who have taken up the subject in retirement, and they are well aware that time has its limits.

Some writers choose subjects which appear to have been of outstanding importance in the life of a particular period. They are driven by a desire to answer certain pressing questions, rather than to use a particular body of evidence. This means that themes may be deliberately chosen for which the evidence is dangerously thin or difficult to interpret: for example the recreational life of ordinary townsmen and countrymen, the nature of religious beliefs, or the effectiveness of education. Nor will we necessarily agree with each others' priorities: while Margaret Spufford, for instance, places considerable emphasis on religious beliefs, Glanmor Williams pleads for more study of the local alehouse.[22]

Equally it is possible to choose much smaller topics, such as the history of a single business or farm, a family or even an individual. Good examples are Mrs Newman's charming account of a single marriage which resulted in the birth of twenty-one children, or D. J. Rowe's study of an enterprising family of farmers in Northumberland.[23] Church guides have been written for generations, but even today only a small minority of churches and chapels are adequately covered.[24] A newer form of local interpretation, of which we need many more examples, is the 'trail'. Having selected an interesting and varied route, to be followed on foot or by car, the writer must briefly discuss the general character of the area and draw attention to some of the finer details which are often overlooked by visitors and even residents. Luckily for the development of local studies, this kind of work is now quite likely to receive the active encouragement and co-operation of planners, education authorities and tourist boards. Many more aids of this kind will have to be written if we are to escape from the present 'siege' mentality which concentrates on outstanding buildings, landscape features and monuments, but neglects the less obvious visual history which is all around us and increasingly vulnerable. The average person's visual awareness is still woefully undeveloped, and this is one major reason why local history does not enjoy the public and official prestige it deserves.

However, a great danger lies in all this specialisation. Academic divisions do not reflect the past itself, but are caused by a professional emphasis on particular themes or kinds of evidence; they are what J. H. Hexter usefully called 'tunnel history'.[25] The local historian's task, admittedly within narrower geographical limits, is to provide as broad and synoptic a view of the past as he can. In these days of ever-increasing specialisation and fragmentation, he puts the emphasis on integration and synthesis. To use a medical simile, he is a general practitioner rather than a specialist; certainly he will draw on the work of specialists, read their journals and even contribute to them, but his concern with the life of the whole community usually gives him a more integrative and reconciling role. For example, the study of an agricultural estate in the eighteenth century usually leads one to discuss local population trends, the varying distribution of wealth, the problem of poverty, the occurrence of domestic industries and improvements in transport, marketing and banking. Whatever the chosen topic, we as local historians want to relate it to the life of the wider community in a way which does not attract the average specialist working in his 'tunnel'. This is probably the most important educational value which can be claimed for the study of local history.

To develop the subject more deeply, a small number of professional writers have recently attempted what is called 'total history'. This is not the approach adopted in the average 'parish history' or 'town biography' which usually ranges over long periods of time in a selective, sometimes miscellaneous, way. On the contrary it is an attempt to show how a community worked *as a whole* and how its constituent parts interwove in the complex texture of local life. The aim, however impossible it sounds, is to study 'life ... in its entirety'.[26] In practice such an ambitious and complex task can only be attempted for relatively short periods. The first book to acknowledge this new objective of total history was Margaret Spufford's *Contrasting communities* (1974) which is mainly concerned with the sixteenth and seventeenth centuries. Here we see a local historian deliberately reacting against the increasing specialisation of other historical colleagues. More recently, Alan Macfarlane has stressed the value of linking up scattered references to as many individuals as possible within a given community. For this purpose he sees twelve categories of documents as central, including parish registers, wills and court rolls.[27] Although that may sound 'total' enough, Barry Stapleton has now shown that, after laboriously reconstituting families from parish registers, one can still weave in personal information from over sixty other kinds of records.[28] This approach is clearly going to make enormous demands on the organising ability and patience of historians and it remains to be seen what effect it will have on the actual writing of history. Even if we regularly achieve a thematic coverage and a search for sources which are close to 'total', our eventual interpretations and writing will still have to be imaginative, generalising and therefore 'partial'.

## Group-work

Although most local history is still written by individuals, an increasing amount of work is done by groups. This is particularly evident in the field of adult education, where classes quite commonly turn themselves into research groups working under the direction of a tutor. After a subject has been agreed, basic tasks such as transcribing and analysing can be undertaken, and the difficulties of interpretation thrashed out in discussion. If the ultimate aim is to publish, it is advisable that someone should co-ordinate the work and be in overall editorial control.[29]

Organisations like the Cambridge Group for the History of Population and Social Structure show how professional scholars may also combine to tackle large-scale projects, and at the same time recruit the assistance of part-timers. Many hundreds of local historians have been drawn into the work of the Group, and have assisted by transcribing parish registers and other sources, and by doing preliminary kinds of analysis. The journal *Local Population Studies* is a worthy monument to the continuing co-operation between professionals and amateurs, which in fifteen years has opened up a fascinating and fundamental aspect of local studies.

The great justification of group-work is that it helps to overcome the isolation of much historical research (the pursuit of archaeology, by contrast, is far more gregarious), and harnesses the energies and abilities of those who may not have produced written history by themselves.

11

## Other ways of writing history: aids to research and teaching

Original reconstructions of the past are not the only forms of written history. The value of gathering contemporary evidence for the benefit of future historians has already been mentioned. Another important job is the compiling of indexes: in every part of Britain, the usefulness of many books, articles, reports and journals is reduced by their having no indexes, or only poor ones. When a new index is compiled, preferably subdivided into Subjects, People and Places, it can easily be duplicated, if not actually printed, and should certainly be deposited in local libraries and record offices.

A related problem is that we often lack bibliographical information. Only a minority of English counties has full-scale bibliographies which list all kinds of published material. This is admittedly an enormous task for anyone to undertake, and it still leaves the problem of coping with new and future publications.[30] But we also need to produce shorter, more selective and critical bibliographies for individual counties or regions. For example, students and teachers frequently seek guidance on particular aspects of local life such as agriculture, religion or trade. Which are the main printed sources, whether books or articles? Where are they to be found? What are their strengths and weaknesses? We also need specific advice on what to avoid, including the new books which perpetuate ancient howlers and are based on minimal research.[31] Again, on a national and regional level we need to follow the example of our archaeological colleagues and compile 'abstracts' summarising the contents of books and articles as they appear.[32]

Lastly comes the vital job of preparing 'record' publications. This of course entails the transcribing (and sometimes translation) of original documents which may be of value to scholars and students. At one end of the scale the result may be a full-blown book published by a record society; at the other end we may produce a pack or archive unit, a duplicated set of transcripts, or simply a 'note' in a journal or newspaper. Whatever the document and the form of publication, critical notes should always be added so that the reader can appreciate the character of the original, its provenance, the special information it offers, and the difficulties of its interpretation. For example, it is not hard to predict that the new edition of Domesday Book, now being published with this kind of helpful annotation, will greatly improve the average person's use of that text.[33] Many local historians, instead of dissipating their energies on wide-ranging, miscellaneous histories, would be better advised to publish some of the most telling local documents, with explanatory introductions.[34]

If local history is really to take root at all levels of the educational system, then vastly more work needs to be done on all these basic chores. In this way the confusion and muddle pervading the subject would come under systematic attack, but its precious vigour and diversity would remain unscathed.

# 3. THE SEARCH FOR SOURCES

This aspect of research has been discussed frequently in the last twenty years. Some books, like W. G. Hoskins' *Local history in England* (second edition, 1972) and W. B. Stephens' *Sources of English local history* (1973), are outstandingly helpful and cannot be ignored by anyone working on a new aspect of the subject. On the other hand, we need more guides which concentrate on individual themes, like Dorothy Owen's *Records of the established church in England* (1970), and on individual counties and regions.[35] In the meantime national and local journals continue to mention and popularise a great variety of primary and secondary sources, as they are discovered and developed by specialist historians.

It is not the purpose of this book to discuss the potentialities of particular sources, for the reasons given in the Foreword, but there are five general points about the search for evidence which ought to be mentioned, because they inevitably affect the quality of our writing:

## (a) The storage of information

The local historian must teach himself, or be taught, the elementary techniques of finding and storing information. This starts with the efficient use of contents pages and indexes in printed books, familiarity with the indexes and catalogues kept in record offices and libraries, and an awareness of the conventions behind transcripts, translations and calendars. These are skills which we should all have been taught at school but, alas, seldom were until quite recently. Fortunately archivists and librarians are usually prepared to explain how their reference-systems work – if, that is, they are asked at a convenient moment.

Historians obviously need an efficient and consistent system of note-taking. Many able people never write because their information is badly stored. It is asking for trouble to fill up notebooks with hundreds of miscellaneous facts and references, because the information is, in effect, buried yet again and is not easy to marshall when one comes to write. Admittedly time should not be spent on unnecessary organisation, and many of us in practice improvise rather reluctantly as the material threatens to engulf us.

One of the best methods is that followed by the staff of the Victoria County History. Basically, each discovered 'fact' with its reference and a short heading is put on a separate slip of paper. Slips, all of the same size, can be stored in a filing cabinet or a cheap substitute like shoe-boxes. As the collection grows, it can be sorted and divided into obvious categories by using index cards with appropriate subheadings (Church, Market, Public

Health, etc). When it comes to writing on a particular topic, the relevant slips can be pulled out, perhaps from several subdivisions, then re-read and arranged in a logical order.[36] Slips are preferable to stiff cards because one can run through them quickly, as with bank-notes. As a further refinement some researchers use slips or cards of different colours. Each colour is devoted to a major aspect of the subject, and this may help the process of sorting. Nevertheless, some historians will choose quite different methods: loose-leaf files, card indexes, envelope files and so on. Whatever system is adopted, it must be flexible, easy to sort and capable of both expansion and subdivision.

It is a good idea to have a special section of notes devoted entirely to sources. Every time a major document, article or book is found, a full reference should be made. Thereafter, any information derived from that source and put on separate cards or slips, need only bear an abbreviated reference. Thus, one's section on sources might contain: Martin, E. W., *The shearers and the shorn, a study of life in a Devon community,* Dartington Hall Studies in Rural Sociology, Routledge and Kegan Paul, London (1965). Individual references taken from the same book need only carry: Martin, *Shearers,* p. 155. Needless to say, all quotations and transcripts must be made accurately, so that one does not in any way misrepresent what a source says.

## (b) The use of printed sources

The rapid and welcome development of record offices and the archival profession has deluded some people into thinking that local history is simply the study of original documents: we merely have to look at manuscripts, get them xeroxed and all is revealed. This is a dangerous fallacy, which gives rise to an uncritical worship of documents in certain educational circles. Not only are many documents dull, repetitive and comparatively unrevealing, but the proper use of manuscripts calls for considerable skill and experience. An essential part of that experience is a knowledge of what is already available in print.

The local historian who neglects published material will undoubtedly miss scores of references to his own locality. More important, he will almost certainly fail to show the real significance of his chosen theme, in the contexts of local life and existing knowledge. In fact it is advisable to start with printed evidence, so that one may avoid unnecessary duplication, and can appreciate the state of knowledge surrounding one's chosen subject.

Printed material must be approached with the same caution as manuscripts. We have to overcome the instinctive assumption that if something is printed it is 'right'. For example, transcription and editing have not always been of the high standard we expect today: editors have been known to select, omit, alter, add and translate freely – all without acknowledgement.[37] Even with a perfect transcription, an editor always stands between us and the manuscript. We are reliant on him for our appreciation of the 'archaeological' character of the original: the material of which it is made, its state of preservation, the character of the handwriting, the physical context in which it was found.

In the case of secondary sources, which are interpretations of the past written by other historians, we should approach them as we would a medieval chronicle. They are someone's version of the past, and not in any sense holy writ. Because historians have a duty to interpret, and to use their evidence imaginatively, they often disagree. This may at first sight seem an embarrassment, but disagreements and historical controversies frequently lead to significant advances in knowledge – because scholars drive each other to think again, to analyse sources more deeply, or to seek entirely new evidence.

Appendix 1 on p. 49 gives more information on the primary and secondary sources which can be found in print. Here it must suffice to say that they include histories of counties, towns and parishes; biographies and personal journals; the publications of record societies; official calendars (summaries of documents); lists and indexes of national archives; county journals; volumes of notes and queries; newspapers and parish magazines. The assistance of a good reference librarian who knows the area is of great importance, especially if he or she is dedicated to the task of indexing and extending the collection.

## (c) The gaining of background knowledge

The third point is an extension of the second. We must never forget the value of wide background reading, for local history is, or should be, a comparative discipline. Without background knowledge, we are unable to see the significance of local events; we do not know when they are part of national trends and when they are purely local phenomena. Margaret Spufford has referred to this as 'the problem that ... bedevils or should bedevil all local historians: what is normal?'[38] The local historian must therefore, in spite of his title, be constantly expanding his knowledge of regional and national history. An obvious example of the value of broader reading lies in the effect of national legislation. When a parish is found to have built a workhouse *c.* 1730, we should see it in the light of the Workhouse Test Act, which positively encouraged such developments. Similarly, when we read in sixteenth-century churchwardens' accounts of the removal of screens, images and altars, we have to be aware of the acts, ordinances and injunctions which activated the English Reformation.

The amount of history now being published in the form of books and articles is truly daunting, not to speak of pamphlets, bulletins and newsletters. For the local historian, the problem is compounded by the width of his interests, for he tries to keep in touch with a whole range of specialisations. In practice, our best chance of coping lies in the use of reviews and other bibliographical aids. Most historical journals include reviews; perhaps the most useful for the average local historian are *History* (the journal of the Historical Association) and *The Local Historian* (the journal of the British Association for Local History). Of particular value are articles which review all the latest work in a limited subject, such as Michael Turner's recent survey of work on parliamentary enclosure, or Margaret Gelling's on the use of Anglo-Saxon charters.[39]

## (d) Making human contacts

The student of local history must seek contact with people who may be able to provide him with new information, or to help him with interpretation. We have already mentioned archivists and librarians, but help may also come from economic historians, archaeologists, place-name specialists, genealogists, geographers, botanists and art historians, to mention but a few. Furthermore, we must gain the confidence of any person who may show us documents, lend photographs or recall useful memories. Perhaps the most valuable contacts of all are with other local historians. For example, much information is found by accident, and if we hope that others will note references which may be useful to us, we must be prepared to do the same for them.

Such help clearly depends on good personal relations and on the regular exchange of news and views. If they do not exist already, ways should be found of ensuring that local historians meet and talk, not just in purely local societies but, more importantly, at a county or regional level. In East Anglia for example, the Centre for East Anglian Studies at the University of East Anglia runs a dining club and a series of seminars at which professionals and part-timers discuss their work. Similarly an informal group of local historians drawn from the western half of Suffolk meets four or five times a year at the record office in Bury St Edmunds. These are fairly typical instances of what is needed to keep serious students in touch. The essential point is that an individual who is isolated is inevitably restricting his own development as an historian, and anyone intending to write cannot afford to be without help and support. Naturally, whenever significant help of any kind is received, it should be acknowledged as a matter of courtesy and honesty.

## (e) Physical evidence

The historian's basic task is to interpret verbal statements. These he will find in primary sources written as part of everyday life, in sources which have been printed, in oral evidence which is now firmly recognised as within the historian's province, and in the ever-growing mountain of secondary sources created by generations of historians as a deliberate reconstruction of the past. However, the sensitive local historian will also be conscious of the landscape or townscape which surrounds him, a vast complex of features contributed by successive generations as they adapted the physical environment according to their economic resources and technical ability. This is important evidence in its own right, albeit of a non-verbal kind, and it simply cannot be ignored.

For example, how can someone writing about religious beliefs and worship neglect the fabric and contents of local churches and chapels? In a discussion of living conditions in the past, is it possible to overlook the results of relevant excavations, or domestic buildings and the furniture which they contained? Similarly, can a student of local farming omit all reference to soils, the shape of the land, the changing pattern of fields, and earthworks like lynchets and ridge-and-furrow? Incidentally, certain kinds of 'visual' document such as maps, engravings and old photographs may prove vital in linking the physical world to the main mass of verbal evidence.

Nobody expects the local historian to become a specialist in architectural history or field archaeology, but he must be prepared to consider other forms of evidence and to draw on the expertise and publications of other specialists where they are relevant to his own interests, and where two or more kinds of evidence can be usefully co-ordinated. While recognising the dangers of stepping into unfamiliar territory, we must be flexible enough to follow where our subject leads.

# 4. TRANSCRIBING AND TRANSLATING

Faced with an original document, the historian's first task is to transcribe the written message, or that part of it which he judges to be relevant to his project. In many cases this means no more than careful reading and accurate copying. However, the earlier the document, the more necessary are the skills of the palaeographer, in order to read styles of handwriting which are no longer in use. Even with quite modern documents, a degree of palaeography is needed: for example, the long 's' was still being used in the nineteenth century, and in every generation some individuals have written badly, hurriedly or in a highly idiosyncratic manner.

This book is no place for a detailed discussion of handwriting and its elucidation. Fortunately several publications already explain the different styles which are likely to be found, and related problems such as abbreviations and 'confusibilia'.[40] Even the simplest manuals, like those provided by the Historical Association, are sufficient for the novice who is willing to work.[41] In the last resort, palaeography is not so much taught as learnt. Every stroke of the pen has to be considered, even if it later turns out to be unimportant; in this way one soon realises that it does not pay to jump to conclusions. Here at least the modern copying machine is a blessing, because it enables us to practise at home on documents which we positively want to understand. We can begin with relatively easy examples and then, motivated by success, tackle more demanding ones. Apart from outright misreadings, the commonest mistakes are a failure to give full and accurate references, and a tendency to 'correct' the spelling of the original.[42] Nevertheless, palaeography should not be regarded as an arcane science reserved only for the initiated. In adult classes one usually finds that intelligent people can (after a few weeks' hard work, and with the right pair of glasses) acquire the expertise to read documents back to about 1550; a few go much further and in time become competent medieval palaeographers.

Assuming that it is not possible to use a typewriter in the record office (which is usually the case), one should get into the habit of writing transcripts in a large, clear and well-spaced hand. Otherwise, at a later stage, details may be easily misconstrued. For example, a hastily scrawled transcript often fails to distinguish capital from lower-case letters. As a further aid to clarity, it pays to write transcripts with a hard pencil. In fact, one should never enter a record office without several pencils, a sharpener, a rubber and enough paper of standard size.

If you are stuck over a word, leave it and move on. Quite often the same word appears again, written in a clearer form. Even if not, the mere act of leaving and then returning with a fresh eye often leads to success: what had been a shapeless squiggle now leaps out as a recognisable word. But even the most skilled palaeographer will sometimes be defeated, and must honestly admit his failure by leaving a gap [within square brackets]. Sometimes we may provide a reading but are not entirely sure of it; here a question-mark should be inserted, once again in the interests of honesty and therefore accuracy. In Appendix 2 on p. 51 is a reminder of the basic rules which should be observed when transcribing original documents.

Where documents were originally written in a language other than English, the historian will also have to translate the text. He will certainly do this in his mind as he reads and transcribes his sources, but at a later stage he may also write a formal translation – especially if it enables him to bring a significant document to the attention of a wider audience. Whereas in practising palaeography we are concerned with symbols or characters, in translating we are concerned with the meaning of words. At this point, the complexities of historical interpretation are beginning to appear: our understanding of what the writer meant to convey starts with his choice of words. In practice the 'foreign' language which the local historian is most likely to meet is Latin, which remained in official use in England until 1753. Fortunately we have an outstandingly good dictionary in Latham's *Medieval Latin word-list* (revised in 1965). For those with no knowledge of Latin, or who need to revise the classical Latin of their schooldays, good aids exist in the shape of Eileen Gooder's *Latin for local history* (1961) and that old faithful, B. H. Kennedy's *Shorter Latin Primer*.

Again, an element of translation is always necessary in the reading of any document, even relatively modern ones written in English. This is because words are constantly changing in meaning and emphasis. Just think of the traps waiting for the unwary in words such as the following:

'prevent' which formerly meant 'go before'
'honest' which meant 'decent' or 'serious'
'steeple' which meant 'tower'
'carpet' which meant a 'covering' or 'table cloth'

In addition, documents often contain dialect words and phrases, which have to be understood. Here again, libraries contain valuable reference books such as Joseph Wright's *English dialect dictionary* (six volumes, 1898–1905) and J. O. Halliwell's *Dictionary of archaisms and regionalisms* (two volumes, 1847).

The transcribing of documents leads to the accumulation of great quantities of paper, which then have to be kept under control. Certainly the sheets should be of a standard size and properly filed. One may be tempted to transfer the more important details into a separate card- or slip-index with, of course, appropriate references. Alternatively the long pages of transcription themselves can be given various underlinings, asterisks, marginal headings and notes, so that the most useful information stands out. Such additions should be readily distinguished from the original transcript by, for example, using a different writing material or colour.

## A note on dating

When transcribing a document, the historian must be careful to note any kind of dating, and then to convert it, if necessary, into a modern form. This means learning when the year began in the past (for example, from the late twelfth century until 1752, the New Year in England normally began on Lady Day, March 25th); also the regnal years of kings and queens, the official years of popes, bishops and abbots, and above all the feasts of the medieval church. As a guide through this maze, we fortunately have C. R. Cheney's *Handbook of dates* which first appeared in 1945 and can still be bought from the Royal Historical Society.

To convert a medieval date to the modern style, the following procedure should be followed. Using Cheney's book:

(1) Identify the date of the feast (pp. 43–64).

(2) Convert the regnal year into a calendar year (pp. 13–31).

(3) If, as is usually the case, your date does not fall exactly on the feast day but on 'the Thursday before' or 'the Monday after', note the number given opposite the calendar year, on pp. 13–31. This in turn refers you to a table somewhere between pp. 84 and 155.

(4) Turn to the relevant table, and identify the precise day of the month.

(In Appendix 3 on p. 53 are some dating exercises which can be done with the help of the *Handbook of dates*.)

# 5. ANALYSIS AND SYNTHESIS

'No document and no statement, official or non-official, is beyond question'

G. Kitson Clark, *The critical historian*, p. 80.

A document does not present the historian with straightforward, reproducible 'truth'. Indeed we are doomed to failure if we attempt to write history by stitching together extracts from original sources. At its most basic, a document can only convey someone's *version* of what happened in the past, and it will assuredly mislead anyone who approaches it uncritically and with no sense of its historical context. The historian has a duty to interpret, and find shape in, the past. Therefore he must read and re-read, always pondering on the significance of what he is reading. His main method of analysis is first, to ask questions which are relevant to the evidence and probe for its meaning; and secondly, because the original writers cannot be re-interviewed, to work out as many answers as he can, for himself. His questions will be concerned with both the detail and general character of documents.

The practical historian, whatever his period of study, cannot remain entirely unaware of the science of diplomatic. This has nothing to do with historical figures like Metternich and Kissinger, but is a series of critical techniques for investigating the origins and character of documents – particularly, as the word implies, the official diplomas and charters of the medieval period. The essential point is that the questions which a diplomatic historian might ask about a medieval charter should pass through the mind of any historian faced with original evidence. Who wrote it, or at least what kind of person wrote it? When, if only approximately, was it written? Does its physical character, say the handwriting, fit the alleged date? Are some of the statements second-hand and derived from earlier sources? Is it a copy? Or a copy of a copy? Is it a forgery?

Basically the whole process is a logical enquiry into the internal and external consistency of documents. It is not necessarily a process of weeding-out or rejection. For example, forgeries may contain genuine and valuable information; by contrast genuine documents do not necessarily tell the whole truth and are often most revealing about the writer's state of mind, his prejudices, assumptions and priorities.[43]

In practice one of the most valuable applications of diplomatic technique is in identifying the work of early historians and antiquaries. The manuscripts of such people are often unsigned and undated; moreover at a later date they were frequently dispersed, re-arranged, cut up, copied and edited. In every county an enormous task of identification, re-sorting and editing remains to be done. A dramatic recent example is Diarmaid

McCulloch's work on the so-called 'Chorography of Suffolk'. This manuscript survey had been written by an unknown person in about 1600, but was unfortunately cut up into several hundred fragments and pasted into many scrapbooks. Later these books were sold and dispersed. The modern editor was able to recognise the fragments by the handwriting and content, and to restore the original text almost completely.[44]

So far as the contents of a document are concerned, a whole succession of questions, general and particular, will arise in the mind of the critical historian as he attempts to 'squeeze' out its meaning. For example:

(1) What parts of the document reflect the personality of the writer (his temperament, knowledge or lack of it, his interests, emotions and prejudices)?

(2) What parts, if any, are determined by administrative procedures (see p. 24) or by the conventions of the period?

(3) How far is the document apparently based on firsthand experience; or derived at second or third hand? What parts appear to be guesswork and opinion?

(4) Does the document contain information that can be corroborated in other sources? Does it contain any unique information?

(5) Do the contents fit current historical opinion; or do they amplify or modify that opinion?

(6) How far can the contents be assessed in terms of truth, ambiguity, omission, distortion and falsehood? (In a single document, one or all of these qualities can appear.)

Questions of this kind are inevitable, though they will not necessarily take exactly the same form as the examples given above. After such an investigation, the historian should be in a position to judge his document's strengths and weaknesses (see example on p. 60). The questions themselves will not normally appear in what an historian writes, but his carefully weighed answers to them will undoubtedly colour the use he makes of the document in a final, overall interpretation.

Central to all this probing is an attempt to enter the mind of the original writer. What did he mean by certain words and phrases? How did he know that fact? Of more general interest, what were his motives and preoccupations when he wrote? Such enquiries do not constitute a secret method known only to professionals; they are the kinds of question which will occur to any curious and intelligent person, or which any good teacher will try to stimulate in the minds of his students when a text is being studied. The whole purpose of this critical exercise is to probe the document for its real meaning (as opposed to its stated meaning), and for its real historical significance in the context of a particular period.

Most documents come from an administrative system which had its own special procedures and terminology. These may not be immediately obvious when the historian first deals with a new category, but with experience he learns what kinds of information to expect and the language which was normally employed. Among other things, he comes to appreciate 'common form', the recurrent words and phrases which say more about the administrative system than about the individual case. When, for example, a late medieval will mentions money bequeathed to a parish church 'for tithes and offerings forgotten', it is not commenting on the life of that particular testator, but is using a normal formula for the period. So in practice the answers to many critical questions will depend on the width of our experience and the depth of our background knowledge. Alternatively, for the beginner, it will depend on getting the right kind of advice, either from an experienced historian or from a suitable publication.

## Methods of analysis

When dealing with a long complicated document, or with several documents of the same kind, the historian is inevitably handling large quantities of paper, whether in the form of notes, or xerox copies, or printed pages. He is therefore forced by the sheer mass of detail to process it in a pre-arranged and systematic way. Many different methods are possible, ranging from elementary to computerised, but they are all intended to sift and sort so that helpful distinctions and comparisons can be built up. When all the information on a particular point has been assembled, the historian is in a much better position to make judgements and calculations, and thus turn the corner from analysis to synthesis.

To analyse the contents of documents, we must first design a series of connected, penetrating questions. Thus, in the case of probate inventories we may ask: how many rooms did local houses contain? How were rooms named? How many rooms were heated? Is it possible to reconstruct the plans of ground floors and first floors? And so on. Our questions are not necessarily purely 'factual'; they often contain distinctions, assumptions and interpretative judgements which have already formed from our reading of the sources. For example, we presume that the presence of fire-irons in a room implies a fireplace; we are not told as much and could be wrong (*see Appendix 4 on p. 58*).

24

Questions on their own are not enough. To answer them comprehensively we must also construct a system for handling all the verbal and numerical detail in documents. A common method is to draw up a form, table or series of columns where details of interest can be noted or counted in the appropriate place. For example, the Cambridge Group for the History of Population supplies three different forms, each with a distinctive colour, for counting baptisms, marriages and burials in parish registers. This also reminds us that, for any particular document or group of documents, more than one analysis may be devised. To return to the example of inventories, we may compile a form for household furniture, itemising beds, tables, chairs and so on; another for stock-in-trade such as the contents of shops and the tools used by craftsmen; a third may be devoted to various kinds of crops and animals; and a fourth to luxuries such as glassware, clocks and objects of silver. Another proven method is to build up special card- or slip-indexes, so that detail from earlier notes or transcripts can be reorganised according to subjects, people and places. For example, an index of personal or topographical names can be abstracted from transcripts of court-rolls and charters. Of all forms of analysis, perhaps the most valuable are those which conflate information from different kinds of document. Regional historians, for instance, regularly devise forms which bring together, for named individuals, evidence from wills, inventories, parish registers, hearth-tax returns, rate-books and so on. (*For examples, see Appendix 4 on pp. 54–59*).

No fixed rules govern these choices. Some people give considerable thought to methods of analysis before they start a project, while others improvise as they go along. No two people will draw up forms of analysis which are identical, and there is no reason why they should: documents are infinitely variable, and historians themselves have different priorities. A method has to be found which is appropriate to each task: it must be large enough in scale to wring useful generalisations from all the relevant detail, but not so elaborate as to have almost as many headings as the document has details. The easiest documents to process are those which have standardised layouts, like tax returns and parish registers; the most difficult are those which are variable and unpredictable in content, like letters and personal journals.

An important advantage of systematic analysis is that it facilitates the making of mathematical calculations. Certain categories of document contain many numbers, such as rentals and accounts, while others present verbal information in such a repetitive way that it can be easily quantified, as with the lists of voters' names in poll-books. The word 'cliometrics' has already been coined to describe the mathematical revolution within history, and manuals are now available which encourage historians to become more numerate.[45] Of course mathematics must not be allowed to obscure the essential humanity of the subject, but at the same time we must not neglect any genuine opportunity of giving our work greater precision.

The table shown below is a single but effective example of analysis and calculation. It comes from Robert Newton's study of Victorian Exeter, and shows the composition of the corporation from 1836–47. The sources were directories, voters' lists, council minutes and newspapers. Similar breakdowns for later periods gave significant comparisons, and showed how the composition of the council was changing as the century wore on.

### OCCUPATIONS OF MEMBERS OF THE EXETER CITY COUNCIL
### 1836–47

| | |
|---|---|
| Wine and spirit mercht., brewer, hotel prop., innkeeper, maltster, hop merchant | 16 |
| Attorney | 16 |
| Builder, auctioneer, timber mercht., surveyor | 8 |
| Doctor, surgeon | 7 |
| Merchant, dealer | 5 |
| Editor, paper mfr., printer | 5 |
| Banker | 4 |
| Draper, mercer, tailor | 4 |
| Currier, leather mercht., boot and shoe mfr., tanner | 4 |
| Ironmonger | 4 |
| Druggist | 3 |
| Jeweller, silversmith, watchmaker | 3 |
| Gentleman, retired | 3 |
| Confectioner, baker, caterer | 2 |
| Grocer | 2 |
| Accountant, bookseller, coach mfr., perfumer, postmaster | 5 |
| [TOTAL] | 91 |

[from Robert Newton, *Victorian Exeter* (1968), p. 340]

But the most important benefit to flow from documentary analysis is the discovery of entirely new facts. For example, E. A. Wrigley was able to write that, between November 1645 and October 1646, 392 people died in the Devonshire town of Colyton. He did not read that fact, as such, in any document; he worked it out by analysing hundreds of entries in a parish register. Furthermore, by making certain assumptions about the birth-rate at that time, he calculated that those deaths probably represented about one-fifth of the whole population.[46] So by re-arranging and re-assembling the information in documents, we can create broader, more generalised or 'integrative' facts. These usually prove very valuable in the writing of history because they are a 'boiling down' of detail which could never be used in its original cumbersome form.

## Relating varied sources

Historical research normally involves the use of many different kinds of evidence. Indeed this is welcomed by most people as a means of giving depth and width to a project. Therefore the historian regularly faces the problem of blending information from an assortment of documents, which were written from different points of view and for quite different purposes. Take for example the censuses, tithe awards and directories which are used by students of the nineteenth century. Censuses were organised nationally to provide standardised statistics on population; tithe awards were part of a national movement to rationalise clerical incomes, by establishing a money-rent in lieu of tithe payments in kind; directories were published commercially, in the hope of selling useful information to the principal inhabitants of local towns and villages. Therefore, evidence drawn from these sources varies in range, in depth, in levels of involvement with the subjects described and in reliability. Yet out of this puzzling mixture of statements and opinions, the historian has to reconstruct, as best he can, what the past was like.

Where points of contact exist, we are naturally keen to discover how far sources seem compatible and mutually supporting, and how far they seem discordant. This is not to isolate some documents as 'true' and others as 'false': we are embarked on a far more subtle and hazardous process than that, which is the very heart of historical interpretation. In our minds we are allowing documents to adjust to, and illuminate, each other so that we become increasingly conscious of their relative strengths and weaknesses, and can begin to construct an overall picture. Census returns, for example, give us some detail about every man, woman and child in a given community (names, relationships, ages, occupations and birthplaces), but they can be positively misleading about certain family relationships or the occupations followed by wives and children. They will describe some men as

27

farmers, and even mention their total acreages and the number of men they employed, but they will not reveal where each man's land lay. By contrast, a tithe award with its map will show with precision who owned and who tenanted every field in a parish. However, in its turn, it may be quite vague about the number of tenants in a tightly built-up area and precisely which cottages or tenements they occupied.

In spite of such difficulties, these two kinds of source are often compared and interwoven, especially when they are close in date. For example, they form the basis of 'house repopulation', a technique used to discover where individuals and families lived in nineteenth-century communities. The strongly topographical evidence of tithe awards and maps is deliberately put against the much more personal detail of census returns.[47] The normal point of contact between the sources lies in personal names: the head of a household mentioned in a census enumerator's book may be repeated in a list of owners or tenants in the tithe award. Once links have been made, it may be possible to see not only where families lived and where they held land, but where particular classes, occupations and even ethnic groups tended to congregate within a village or town, and what living conditions were like in houses and streets which have survived.[48]

Such analyses and comparisons mean that the historian does not play a merely passive role, pasting together snippets from different sources. He has to think hard, 'argue' internally with his sources and use his creative imagination until he is fully aware of the quantity and quality of his varied evidence. This awareness, resulting from a curious sort of verbal chemistry, is the basis of our imaginative reconstruction of the past, and will form a substantial part of anything we write. Our interpretation will certainly be more complicated than if we had used only one source, but at the same time it will be a more realistic reflection of the complicated truth. (*Another, more intricate example may be seen in Appendix 5, Part C on p. 61.*)

One of the special fascinations of local history is that it often presents the opportunity of weaving in various kinds of non-verbal evidence – such as domestic buildings, churches, funerary monuments, tools and implements, archaeological sites, industrial remains, field-systems and a host of other landscape features. For example, several years ago I was thrilled to find that an attractive green lane along our parish boundary, now merely a farm track and footpath, was described in a sixteenth-century manorial survey as 'The Quenes High Waye' leading to a market town ten miles away. It is in fact part of a broad drove-road which linked two interdependent agricultural regions. But exciting though this kind of co-ordination can be, one often encounters problems.

Words and physical remains are very different kinds of evidence, and sometimes they appear to be in conflict. They therefore have to be carefully studied, each in its own terms, before they can be convincingly associated. Generally these apparent conflicts disappear when we realise that we have wrongly or inadequately interpreted one or both kinds of evidence. For example, in 1860 a Suffolk parson named Richard Cobbold wrote of his Rectory, 'I built this house in the year 1827'. An inspection of the house soon reveals a substantial timber-framed structure dating from the sixteenth or seventeenth centuries, to which a large brick wing had clearly been added in the nineteenth century. The building therefore discloses a far more complicated structural history than Cobbold's rather loose language suggests; meanwhile the written statement itself usefully uncovers his personal attitude to the old-fashioned parsonage which he had inherited and thought beneath his dignity. This, in a minor way, is the sort of problem and opportunity which Barrie Trinder had in mind when he wrote about historical and archaeological evidence coming 'fruitfully into conflict'.[49]

# 6. THE END PRODUCT

'There are three parties. . . . to the process of interpretation:
the interpreter, the mind he interprets, and the mind to whom
he interprets.'

        A. E. Levett, *Studies in manorial history* (1938) p. 8.

Do not postpone writing for too long, because it can so easily be for ever. Some people prevaricate by saying that they have not finished their research, but this is an excuse rather than an explanation. No piece of history is ever complete and definitive for all time, yet in practice there comes a point beyond which you are unlikely to find evidence which will substantially alter your interpretation – so you should take the plunge. Indeed the longer writing is delayed, the more difficult it can get to organise a formidable mass of material. As Finberg said, in quoting R. H. Worth, 'One always writes too soon; but if one puts it off, one may not write at all'.[50]

Once a relatively self-contained corpus of documents has been studied and analysed, the agonising process of writing can and should begin. Already ideas of interpretation will have formed in the mind, some idea of the argument it is wished to present and the order of its unfolding. At this stage the importance of individual documents and published sources recedes: the historian is preoccupied with the shaping of *his own* vision of the past, to make it as accurate and penetrating as possible, and yet at the same time personal and truly unique. This duality makes the historian's task fascinating and, at the same time, extremely demanding.

The overall design of a piece of writing must be considered with great care. The challenge is to divide the subject into manageable, reasonably self-contained lengths, and in so doing to emphasise significant aspects of the past. The normal kind of division is by chapter, but we must also remember that each chapter contains logical subdivisions, whether or not they are distinguished by special subheadings. Three main possibilities leap to mind. First, one may decide that the main divisions of a text should be *thematic;* then within each chapter one might adopt a chronological approach. This is the pattern used by H.M. Colvin in his history of Deddington in Oxfordshire: his chapters bear such titles as The Parish and its Boundaries, Local Government, Fields and Farmers, The Parish Church. Alternatively one may decide to make the main divisions *chronological,* and within them to deal with different topics in turn. This is how most parish histories have been written, with sections on The Middle Ages, The Tudor Period, The Seventeenth Century and so on. Finally one may choose to interweave themes and periods in a more subtle manner. Thus W. G. Hoskins in his *Midland peasant* moves forward in a steadily chronological way, but deliberately emphasises major themes in the titles of chapters: The Medieval Manor, 1066–1509; The Medieval Village and its Fields; The Peasant Farmer in the Tudor Period; The Enclosure, 1764–66. This often seems the best approach but, frankly, it is impossible to lay down firm rules. Everything depends on the subject and the balance of its constituent parts.[51]

Considerable thought must also be given to the order in which the argument unfolds. Analysis has shown that three main elements should be present: *narrative* which gives the sequence of events, and emphasises time and change; *description* which conveys what happened at a particular time; and *analysis* which is the attempt to explain why things happened, and to show how events are connected.[52] Every student of history has to learn that he must not write long passages of narrative or description, and then as an afterthought insert small pieces of analysis. He must keep all three dimensions in regular play, as he both describes and explains the past. Other kinds of balance must be preserved as well: the reader should be moved frequently, backwards and forwards, between detail and broad generalisation, between facts and judgements, between the locality and the wider world. (*See Appendix 6 on pp. 67–70.*)

Another vital ingredient is *comparison*. Thus, in describing how a town was governed in the seventeenth century, we may profitably compare it with other towns at the same period, or compare it with the same town in earlier and later centuries. This kind of movement through space and time not only gives life to a text, but helps to measure the significance of what is being studied. The need to compare, and to place work in a wider framework, explains the frequent use of 'general' sources like lay subsidies, hearth-tax returns, poll books and returns of expenditure on the poor. Their great virtue, apart from the fact that they are often in published form, is that they survey whole areas or counties, at one time and in a reasonably consistent manner. Therefore they enable the historian to judge local communities *relative to each other,* whether in terms of population, housing, wealth, social composition, employment or whatever. (*See Appendices 1 and 4, pp. 49 and 56.*)

*The ultimate aim in writing is to design an unbroken chain of systematic argument, which not only describes what happened in the past but almost simultaneously tries to explain why it happened.* This can only be done when the evidence has been wholly assimilated, and when the logic of an historical interpretation has been thoroughly worked out. So many pieces of writing have only gone so far towards this objective; they are disjointed impressions and anecdotes rather than logical discussions. A common symptom is the 'slab technique' whereby passages dealing with national history are dropped at intervals into the story of local life, but inadequately related to it. Ironically, therefore, while many of us are reluctant to start writing, we then spend insufficient time on the job and publish too soon!

## Preliminary notes and the first draft

Before tackling any particular chapter or section, you should physically spread out all the relevant information you have – whether in the form of slips, cards, lengthy transcripts, analyses, indexes or whatever. The mere act of finding and re-reading these bits of evidence helps to clarify their relative significance, and may lead immediately to the rejection of items which are inessential. Furthermore, while the notes are spread out on a table, you can experiment as long as you like with their arrangement in the hope of finding a satisfying sequence which can form the basis of a piece of writing.

With all the evidence fresh in the mind and physically arranged, you are in a position to rough out a few notes which will establish the main twists and turns of your historical argument, and can later be expanded into a first draft. The actual length of these vital notes is a matter of personal choice: some fluent and practised writers find it sufficient to jot down the main ideas behind a whole chapter, but most of us will probably prefer to sketch out the text in greater detail, perhaps down to the level of individual paragraphs. (*See Appendix 6 on pp. 63–70.*)

The shape of this book has probably given the impression of a linear system in which one clear-cut stage succeeds another. In real life, however, research and writing often overlap. Ideas are sometimes written up while documents are being studied, and are later slotted into the main text. Alternatively, once embarked on writing, historians are frequently driven back to do more research, because the coverage is in some way incomplete or unsatisfying. Moreover, documents have the irritating habit of turning up late in the day, and this too can lead to revision. In practice, therefore, you may experience a constant interplay between your work on sources, your background reading of other historians and your actual writing.

The question is often asked, for whom are we writing? The answer must partly depend on the kind of history being produced. An article for a learned journal will have a form suitable for one kind of audience, while a newspaper article, or a privately published parish history, will be designed for a different readership. Yet the differences should only be of degree, not of kind: they should merely concern the length and elaboration of the argument. One of the most useful precepts we can remember is that *all* kinds of written history should assume intelligence on the part of the reader, but not necessarily knowledge. Regrettably, many publications, especially of the local sort, talk down to the reader or assume that he only wants to be entertained. In fact, the complexities of local history inevitably demand effort of both writer and reader.

The preliminary sketch provides the raw material and stimulus for a first draft. While the ideas flow, be thankful and write quickly. Leave plenty of space between lines, because you will inevitably alter the text as you write. Unless you happen to be a competent typist, you will probably find that the fastest method of writing is by hand. It is vitally important that at this stage you do not torment yourself by reflecting on the niceties of style; even jargon is forgivable in a first draft. Do not fall for the temptation of stopping every few minutes and reading over what you have just written. This may occasionally be useful to confirm a train of thought, but can easily become a sort of nervous paralysis which seriously delays progress. At all costs keep the text moving and – in spite of the temptation – do not get bogged down with fine detail. Writing quickly you may produce very inflated, repetitive prose; on the other hand, you may miss out parts of the argument and slide over complications. These defects do not matter because they can be repaired later. On a similar point, W. G. Hoskins advises that a writer should leave off a day's work 'without completely exhausting the subject in hand'.[53] The next day he can pick up the threads with far less trouble than if he were beginning a totally new subject. It follows that, if time is limited, writing should be done little and often, rather than in widely-spaced bursts of activity.

Do not forget to number your pages as you write, or you will be in a muddle by the end of the day. While notes and transcripts are still spread out on a table, it is also advisable to put in as many references as possible. You should not worry if your original sequence of numbers for references is later broken: you are very likely to delete some references which on maturer reflection seem inessential, and to insert new ones like (32A) and (32B). A final sequence of numbers, synchronised in both text and end-notes, can be produced when everything else has been completed: if you do this job too soon, you are in danger of producing two or more conflicting series of numbers. Similarly, references should not be re-copied unnecessarily, because errors will inevitably creep in. If the details for a reference are not to hand as you write, then leave a gap which can be filled later, and do not break that precious flow of thought and effort.

However, in spite of all this emphasis on continuous effort, one major exception must be allowed. If it proves difficult to write on a particular subject, one should temporarily abandon the attempt – certainly for several days – and then return with a fresh mind. By this device the solution is often found which at first seemed so elusive.

Try to make sure, even at this early stage, that each paragraph is reasonably self-contained, and built around one major idea. Also see that it connects logically with its neighbours, and thus appears to be part of an overall, planned discussion. The surest signs of sloppy preparation and careless writing are overlong, rambling paragraphs which have no obvious shape or core of ideas.

A first draft will usually be very untidy with insertions, crossings-out and arrows reversing the order of sentences; this is the inevitable consequence of trying to express complicated thoughts as quickly as possible. In a second draft you can refine and polish to your heart's content. Indeed you may not be satisfied until a third or fourth draft is written and, even then, may be carrying out small-scale modifications for months.

## Some guidelines for writing

Nobody can give a detailed blueprint for writing history, but a few general principles can be hazarded:

(1) Above all, one must produce history which is humane in both content and style. The central concern must be with people – thinking, sentient human beings in all their diversity. Even though mention is inevitably made of documentary sources, methods of analysis, statistics and the physical world, these ought never to be regarded as ends in themselves but as merely contributing to the complex story of man. Yet the opposite is frequently the case. As John Marshall has remarked, 'Plenty of people have written about the Poor Law, but very few, convincingly, about the poor!' Similarly economic historians often write as if their concepts have no connection with real life. Prices, for example, are not simply figures: they show the value which people put on commodities, and the historian's language should reflect this. In the study of local history, we are mainly concerned with ordinary, relatively obscure and 'unsung' people, and trying, with compassion, to reconstruct something of their lives. The local historian has no greater reward than to be able to show that the lives of ordinary people had meaning and dignity; that they were individuals and certainly did not regard themselves as equals, socially or morally; that they, like the 'great' and 'famous', had hopes and fears, joys and pain, achievement and failure.

Because of the nature of historical evidence, we often concentrate on fairly large groups of people, for example, those who pursued the same occupation, had a common faith, or regarded themselves as belonging to the same class, but we must also seize those rarer opportunities of talking about individual men, women and children. This does not mean throwing in every personal titbit we happen to know: simply that where we have something important to say, we should express it as humanely as possible. 'I am an historian', said Marc Bloch. 'Therefore, I love life.'(54)

34

(2) Interpretation must involve the selection and emphasis of those issues which seem most significant. We ought, in other words, to give shape to the past, and not present a mere catalogue of miscellaneous facts and trivial anecdotes. The shorter the study, the more selective it should be. It does not follow that we should only write about the unusual or the dramatic, like those wretched murders which feature prominently in so many local histories. Murders may actually be of some importance, but only when they are embedded in a wider study of crime, law or morality. In a balanced account, we must also stress the typical and the ordinary. Indeed the long-term trends and regularities of life are usually more important than isolated events.

(3) Unfortunately, many local historians do not exert sufficient control over their evidence. They dutifully but unimaginatively describe each document in turn, and thus allow the sources to shape their thinking and writing (see p. 71). To write well, the historian must remain firmly in charge and draw out the evidence which suits his own critical and imaginative purposes. At times this may indeed mean bringing certain documents under very close scrutiny; usually, however, the evidence is kept at greater distance as we survey clusters of miscellaneous sources, and use only those parts which seem telling and relevant to our view of the past. (*See Appendix 5 on pp. 60–62.*)

(4) As with the analysis of individual documents, the best way of giving shape to writing is by posing intelligent questions. How many people lived here? Was the population rising or falling? How did people earn their livings? Were there marked differences of wealth? How did the community govern itself?

Primary enquiries of this kind lead to others of a more detailed nature. Alan Rogers' book *Approaches to local history* is especially useful for its discussion of the questions which arise from detailed work. Here, for example, are the ways in which he suggests a local historian might probe into the subject of religion:

> '... how important was religion among the community? How widespread was its acceptance? What proportion of the population was among the active or its more formal adherents? ... What religious organisations did they enjoy? When and how did they originate? And what were their relations, the one to the other? What sort of persons predominated within each organisation? And ... what sort of activity did they engage in? Were they inward looking or "full of good works"? What attempts did they make to deal with the problems of their contemporary society, to reach those outside?'[55]

In a piece of published history, such questions need not be overtly stated; normally in fact they are not. The real value of an historian's questions is that they guide his thoughts as he writes. Then, as his text unfolds, it will contain strong threads of logic and order, of analysis and discussion.

(5) It follows that the historian must not bombard the reader with details, but select those which best illustrate significant issues and trends. Furthermore, he must always make detail count by explaining its relevance. By doing these things he escapes, as Lionel Munby has expressed it, from the prison of his own knowledge.[56] Selection also implies rejection: you cannot expect to use all your evidence in writing, however painfully it was gathered or joyfully found. Although an historical synthesis should be based on all relevant evidence, many facts and references will turn out to be inessential. On the other hand, you must certainly not suppress any evidence which is inconvenient or contradictory to your case.

(6) As has been said, a strong chronological thread must run through any historical writing, because history records the passage of time and the changes which time brings. Indeed pieces of pure narrative frequently introduce events in strict chronological order. Nevertheless, time must not become a strait-jacket to the design of an historical argument. It is sometimes far more effective, both for historical and literary reasons, to move around chronologically: many a biography, for example, begins with the death or funeral! (*See example on p. 80.*)

(7) Quotations, either from original sources or from the work of other historians, can be a highly effective device in writing because they introduce new, fresh voices. They must be long enough to make a telling point, but not so long as to bore the reader and unbalance the text. Local historians often use excessively long quotations (*See Appendix 7(I) on pp. 71–73.*) Presumably they do this in the hope of giving authenticity to their work, but in fact they merely expose their own failings. In Finberg's words, 'there is no better way of unnerving the average reader at the outset than to hurl a chunk of Domesday at him, without any explanation of its terminology or so much as a hint that scholars are not altogether certain what some of the entries mean'.[57] Yet (it is worth saying a second time) the crude stitching together of extracts from original sources is the most common mistake in the writing of local history. Quotations can greatly improve the texture of historical writing, but they must be used judiciously and, like jewels in a

crown, must be securely embedded in a text which explains them. Needless to say, all quotations should be fully and accurately referenced (see p. 88). It is a serious crime to use somebody else's words or ideas without acknowledgement.

(8) Given the nature of historical evidence, our knowledge will always contain uncertainties, doubts and gaps. These must be acknowledged with candour. Good written history is liberally sprinkled with actual or implied question-marks, because the historian can never expect to uncover the whole truth. (The related question of what language the historian should employ to express complicated judgements and degrees of possibility and probability, is discussed on p. 41).

(9) As a person aiming to study the past objectively, the historian must certainly try to keep his own beliefs and prejudices under strict control. On the other hand, his contemporary involvements will inevitably influence what he writes, and he should not be afraid of revealing them. It is better to write one-sided and partial history, and to be frank about it, than to attempt any form of deceitful indoctrination, political, religious or otherwise. When Edward Thompson writes that 'Enclosure... was a plain enough case of class robbery, played according to fair rules of property and law laid down by a parliament of property-owners and lawyers', he may not be achieving the highest standards of historical impartiality, but he is at least giving us a useful and thought-provoking way of looking at a familiar problem.[58] However objective we try to be, our writing remains an expression of ourselves; it should therefore show personality.

## Producing a final draft

> Caxton's tribute to Chaucer: 'He combined his matters in short, quick and high sentences, eschewing prolixity, casting away the chaff of superfluity, and chewing the picked grain of sentence . . .'

> 'No language has better ingredients than English; no language has ever been more monstrously ill-treated and deformed by vandals and incompetents.'
> Kenneth Hudson, *Dictionary of diseased English* (1977), p. xiii.

In the second draft, and later ones if they prove necessary, a writer is normally concerned with the refinement of his prose so that it is clear, direct and elegant. Again there is no formula for success, but plenty of examples show what to aim at, and what to avoid.

(1) We must be prepared, if necessary, to recast the first draft extensively. This may mean changing the order of words, altering the voice and mood of verbs, or re-structuring whole paragraphs. After all, it is usually possible to write the same sentence in several, fundamentally different ways. (Try it!) One major reason for the ugliness and confusion of much modern writing is the apparent unwillingness of writers to revise first drafts.

(2) In the hope, as they think, of giving their prose greater dignity and weight, many writers complicate their message quite unnecessarily. They actually prefer the complex to the simple, the oblique to the direct, the pompous to the plain; they choose the rare word where the common one would serve better, and they observe Finberg's tongue-in-cheek rule 'never to use one word where you can possibly use four'.[59] To fall for these temptations shows a lamentable disregard for the suffering reader. Heaven knows that historical truth is complicated enough; it must not be further complicated by obscurity of expression. (*For several examples, see Appendix 8 on pp. 76–78.*)

(3) One is frequently dissatisfied with a passage, without knowing exactly what is wrong. This 'inner voice' of criticism should be heeded as it is invariably right. On maturer reflection, one realises that the logic of an argument has not been worked out thoroughly enough; something may be missing, or an idea, though mentioned, may not have been given sufficient weight. A comment which began as a subordinate clause frequently has to be given the status of a separate sentence, or more. On the other hand, it is a common experience to have to prune the first draft. There are always unnecessary words, phrases, sentences and even paragraphs. For example, we often leave behind more of our original mental 'scaffolding' than is strictly needed: 'Now we must turn, as in the last chapter, to the subject of. . . .' Or we may find that we have included facts and ideas which impede the flow of an argument and are better placed in references, footnotes or appendices. The more compact our writing, the more forceful and effective it becomes. With the high cost of modern printing, we cannot afford to waste space as older antiquaries did with their more egotistical and ruminative styles (see No. 5, p. 76). Who was it who said that, if he had had more time, he would have written a shorter book?

(4) Although he may not be writing literature in the strict sense, an historian must always try to give his writing shape, rhythm and style. For example, a first draft may contain too many short words which

have a jerky and percussive effect ('He put it out that at the time he could not come'). Or words may be too repetitive as sounds ('... barely been begun ...'). How often too, important sentences begin with impersonal and unnecessary constructions like 'It can be argued that...' or 'It should go without saying that...'. Every text should be combed for weak colloquial expressions which make language flabby and less direct. The most common of all are probably 'there is ... there were ... it seems that ... it is possible that ...'. A writer who is truly dedicated to the task of communicating must constantly seek opportunities for cutting, tightening and strengthening his prose. Frequently an important word appears early in a sentence, and its effect is then undermined by later, qualifying clauses. Though not an invariable rule, it often helps to reorganise sentences so that the really important words come towards the end, as a sort of climax. Similarly, in giving a string of examples one should keep the most effective until last ('... but above all ...').

We must be prepared to mould and re-mould our writing until it flows with ease and elegance, and until key words and phrases have the prominence and impact which they deserve. In this sense, style is not an optional extra, or a cosmetic: it is part of the basic craft of communicating.

(5) Jargon is a curse in all academic subjects, but it is particularly regrettable in the study of man and human society. Not only does it make communication difficult, but it frequently prevents us from thinking clearly in the first place. For example, we were recently informed that 'the main reason why so many parish registers were unreliable was probably a function of the system of registration'. This kind of circular writing is often caused by the seductive power of words like 'function' and 'situation'. New examples of ugly jargon are regularly coined, usually by professionals who should know better. In recent years we have been asked to swallow: non-migratory mobility, residential propinquity, extra-familial relationships, multi-source nominal record linkage, and many others. It is no accident that those who are in the habit of using jargon, are poor writers anyhow.

A distinction should be made between jargon and technical words. Jargon is unnecessarily obscure and ungainly language, usually characterised by an accumulation of nouns. It is written by members of specialised groups who have no interest in communicating with the outside world – this is why it is totally indefensible in the study of history. By contrast, technical words are coined to describe new methods and concepts, with which traditional language cannot easily cope. They are therefore acceptable in the writing of history, providing they are explained when first used. Thus historians legitimately refer to the 'cost of living index', to 'mean household size' and 'age at first marriage'.

(6) A useful characteristic of the English language is that two or more nouns can be put side by side, with or without hyphens. Phrases like 'income tax' and 'town centre' are a concise form of expression where the earlier nouns play an adjectival role. However, this useful device is being increasingly abused by many writers, especially academics and journalists. Instead of using adjectives, participles and prepositions (particularly that vital little word 'of'), these new barbarians pile nouns together indiscriminately. Published history now teems with coarse and ponderous expressions which are quite unnecessary. One can invariably think of clearer, more elegant and sometimes shorter ways of expressing the point. For example:
> birthplace location analysis (meaning 'the analysis of birthplaces')
> house plan classification types (meaning 'types of house-plan')
> volume analysis completion rate (meaning 'the rate at which volumes were completed')
> labour force participation rates (meaning 'the proportion of people at work')
> case fatality rate (meaning 'the proportion of people infected, who died')
> census data capture sheet (meaning that someone is past redemption).

The fact that some nouns are superfluous shows the basic carelessness of this kind of writing. In languages with a more precise structure, for instance French and Latin, such clumsiness would be impossible, but in English we are witnessing the illiterate abuse of greater freedom.

(7) An undue stress on nouns leads to the devaluing of verbs, and therefore to a lumpiness and obliqueness in the general character of writing. After a few moments of self-criticism, a dull and impersonal phrase like '... in a period of acute population pressure and increasing conversion to arable' will re-emerge as '... in a period when the population grew fast and ever more land was being ploughed'. So often nowadays, direct and strong verbs are rejected in favour of abstract and passive ones. One infallible sign that we have fallen into this trap is the persistent use of abstract nouns such as: factor, structure, pattern,

condition, activity, tendency, index and, above all, *situation*. (See No. 13 on p. 77.)

(8) The historian has a duty to choose words which are as precise and concrete as possible. Every student is warned not to use vague terms like 'the people' or 'progress' when it is usually possible to say which people he has in mind, and what kind of progress. Similarly one must beware of historical labels such as 'The Middle Ages' and 'capitalism' which can mean different things to different men.

Linguistically and stylistically the greatest difficulty arises when we have to express judgements and opinions – with which history abounds. This is why the literature is full of adverbs like 'perhaps' and 'probably', of adjectives like 'uncertain' and 'ambiguous', and of phrases like 'the evidence suggests . . .' or 'on balance, it seems likely that . . .'. The use of numbers has certainly given more precision to historical writing, but our main tools are still words, and they have to be used as responsibly and accurately as possible. Indeed we face a new challenge today: that of developing a literary style which will express the increasing numeracy of our interpretations. (*See Appendix 10 on p. 82.*)

(9) Having written a passage, and having at great effort got as close as possible to your final draft, put the manuscript away for a fortnight or more. On re-reading it, you will invariably see imperfections which you had previously overlooked. This is also the opportunity for thinking about small but important details. Often we need to correct the order of words ('He was one of seven invited people to the meeting') or bring together phrases which imply time or place ('In 1578 John Smith left £200 when he died') or make sure that we do not unnecessarily mix constructions in the same sentence ('In 1440 Edward Brown left his tenement to his son Thomas, and his daughter Jane was to have £5'). One must also choose carefully between the definite and indefinite articles: 'the' is grossly overused and frequently retards the flow of writing. In fact both articles are overused. Why, for example, do historians refer so much to 'the' plague or 'a' plague when neither introduction is necessary? This is also the time to think of the value of linking words such as 'however' and 'yet', or of words which give emphasis like 'indeed' and 'particularly'. We all overuse certain words, expressions and constructions, and may not realise it until we re-read the text after an interval, or until someone else points it out. Alternatives can usually be found in Roget's *Thesaurus* or standard

41

dictionaries. At this stage, too, all references should be carefully checked for errors and inconsistency.

(10) When a text is finished, and before it is published, it should be read by at least three other people – but do not be surprised if their reactions differ, or even contradict. One reader should be a specialist who has experience or qualifications relevant to the subject, and another should be a non-specialist who can be relied upon to object if the writing is unclear. How sad it is that many local historians, having sought help in the earlier stages of their research, publish their findings without inviting any further comment.

## References

These are a vital part of the mechanism of history. They are not, as some amateurs think, a form of masochistic generosity whereby we give away our best sources and hand a cudgel to our enemies. Nor are they a self-indulgent and unnecessary luxury, as some second-rate publishers think. On the contrary, to give references is simply to declare one's good faith. Because history is based on the interpretation of evidence, a writer must indicate the nature of that evidence, and give the reader the chance of consulting it for himself. Not to do so is to invite suspicion and criticism; this is why so much published history, of the local kind, is ignored or rejected by professional historians.

Of course readers will use references in different ways. In many cases they are only interested in broadening their background knowledge by reading what other historians have said. On the other hand, those who are carrying out research on related subjects will want the opportunity of consulting the original sources and studying the writer's use of them. Because no piece of history can ever be 'the final word', references are therefore an invitation to keep the debate open and to take the work further. In this sense, history is a co-operative venture, though historians may 'co-operate' who work in isolation and never meet.

In giving references a balance must be struck. All major facts and opinions, especially if they are important turning-points in the argument, must be supported by full references. On the other hand, the text must not be overloaded so that the reader is left confused or intimidated. Nobody can cope with a reference after each sentence, and in any case many basic facts will never be challenged, for example that Charles II was restored to the throne in 1660 or that Napoleon lost the Battle of Waterloo. Nor should the historian try to prove each point by hurling a great quantity of references at the reader. For example, Eric Kerridge's seminal book on the *Agricultural Revolution* is seriously marred by the number and length of its footnotes.

Remember also that several references can be grouped into a single note – providing they are in sequence and do not take up more than a few lines of print. Finally, do not give a direct reference to a source which you have not actually consulted, but only seen mentioned elsewhere. In such cases, the honest policy is to give the primary source 'as quoted in' the secondary.

The traditional form of reference is the footnote which appears at the bottom of the relevant page. Nowadays it is more common to group references at the end of each chapter, or at the end of the whole article or book (end-notes); this method leaves the main text unbroken and certainly makes life easier for typists and printers. References are indicated in the text by a number, with or without brackets, and should be placed, whenever possible, at the end rather than in the middle of a sentence. In the case of footnotes, the sequence of numbers is normally by the page; with grouped references one should have a sequence running through each chapter, article or whole book. To help readers find their place, references at the end of a book should not only be clearly subdivided by chapter (each time giving the number and title) but every column should be headed by a further reference to the relevant pages of the text.

The so-called Harvard system of referencing, often used in scientific periodicals, is not suitable for historical writing. It makes an ugly intrusion into the printed text, for example (Warren, 1951, pl. 5), and unnecessarily duplicates some of the information given in a final bibliography.

*(In Appendix 12 on pp. 88–90 are recommended rules for references and bibliographies.)*

## Appendices

Where a writer judges that transcripts of documents and other background information would be of interest to the reader, but are too bulky for the main text, he may choose to use appendices. These are perfectly acceptable, providing they have a clear relevance to the text.

## A final reminder

It is not the purpose of this book to discuss the problems of actual publishing – how, for example, one finds a printer, negotiates a price, arranges the layout, deals with proofs, organises distribution and so on. These have been mentioned in several general textbooks by W. G. Hoskins, Bernard Jennings, Dorothy Creigh and others, and have been the subject of four articles in *The Local Historian* by James Batley.[60] However, the importance of providing an index must be stressed, because this aid which is vital for the discerning reader is often omitted. When a local historian writes a book, he should compile, or have compiled, an index which is full and well subdivided. Sound guidance will be found in R. F. Hunnisett, *Indexing for editors, Archives and the user, No. 2* (1977).

## Further reading

For those wishing to read further about historical methods in general, the following titles are recommended:

Arthur Marwick, *Introduction to history,* The Open University (1977).

G. Kitson Clark, *The critical historian* (1967).

G. R. Elton, *The practice of history* (1967).

Jacques Barzun and Henry F. Graff, *The modern researcher* (3rd ed. 1977). (This is a highly detailed but fascinating analysis of how research is done, or should be done.)

# REFERENCES

1 In W. G. Hoskins, *Local History in England* (2nd ed. 1972), only five pages out of 235 are concerned with writing. Similarly, in spite of its promising title, R. B. Pugh, *How to write a parish history* (1954) devotes three out of 140 pages to this topic.

2 H. P. R. Finberg, 'How not to write local history' in H. P. R. Finberg and V. H. T. Skipp, *Local history, objective and pursuit* (1967), pp. 71–86.

3 The following books contain substantial amounts of local history, and employ a range of historical techniques, yet all are written by non-historians: John Barrell, *The idea of landscape and the sense of place 1730–1840: an approach to the poetry of John Clare* (1972); Alan Macfarlane, *The family life of Ralph Josselin, a seventeenth-century clergyman: an essay in historical anthropology* (1970); Oliver Rackham, *Trees and woodland in the British landscape* (1976); Jean Robin, *Elmdon – continuity and change in a north-west Essex village, 1861–1964* (1980).

4 Paul Thompson, *The voice of the past* (1978), Chapter 1.

5 A. S. Jasper, *A Hoxton childhood* (1974); *The Island – the life and death of an East End of London community* (1979).

6 As the editor of a national journal, I am no longer amazed to receive articles from university lecturers which contain frequent stylistic failures and spelling mistakes.

7 On the subject of A-level projects, the Cambridge Local Examination Syndicate in 1973 warned teachers that 'it wishes to ensure that projects are not supervised at every stage in their gestation as if they were MA or PhD theses. This means that a teacher should not concern himself with research, drafting, writing and final presentation.' No doubt some teachers are relieved to read this, but are we to assume that the guidance regularly given to postgraduates is not needed by sixth-formers?

8 Geoffrey Elton, foreword in J. Z. Titow, *English rural society, 1200–1350* (1969).

9 Biography and military history are also very popular, but I still think that if we include all forms of published local history (e.g. commercial 'county' magazines, church guides, parish magazines, local newspapers, etc.), it is the most widely read.

10 David G. Hey, *An English rural community: Myddle under the Tudors and Stuarts* (1974). Gough's account is now available as Richard Gough, *The history of Myddle* (Penguin, 1981).

11 Margaret Spufford, *Contrasting communities: English villagers in the sixteenth and seventeenth centuries* (1974); J. R. Ravensdale, *Liable to floods: village landscape on the edge of the fens, AD 450–1850* (1974).

12 Alan Rogers, 'Local and regional history' in *Regional History Newsletter,* No. 3; J. D. Chambers, 'The vale of Trent, 1670–1800'. *Econ. Hist. Rev. Supplements,* No. 3 (1957).

13 K. P. Witney, *The Jutish forest: a study of the Weald of Kent from 450–1380 AD* (1976); R. Fieldhouse and B. Jennings, *A history of Richmond and Swaledale* (1978).

14 A. Hassell Smith, *County and court: government and politics in Norfolk, 1558–1603* (1974). For an attempt at the integrated or 'total' history of a county, see Peter A. Clark, *English provincial society from the Reformation to the Revolution: religion, politics and society in Kent, 1500–1640* (1977).

15 The well-known series published by Hodder and Stoughton on 'The making of the English landscape' consists of county volumes; so does 'The industrial archaeology of the British Isles' published by David and Charles.

16 David Jenkins, *The agricultural community in south-west Wales at the turn of the twentieth century* (1971); Victor Skipp, *Crisis and development, an ecological case study of the Forest of Arden, 1570–1674* (1978); (Ed. Marilyn Palmer), *The onset of industrialisation*, Dept. of Adult Education, Univ. of Nottingham (1977); Marie B. Rowlands, *Masters and men in the West Midland metalware trades before the industrial revolution* (1975); T. J. Raybould, *The economic emergence of the Black Country: a study of the Dudley estate* (1973); J. M. Preston, *Industrial Medway: an historical survey* (1977); P. R. Mountfield, 'The footwear industry of the East Midlands', *East Midland Geographer*, Vol. 3, Nos 22–4; Vol. 4, Nos. 25 & 27; J. K. Walton and P. R. McGloin, 'Holiday resorts and their visitors: some sources for the local historian', *The Local Historian*, Vol. 13, No. 6 (1979), 323–331.

17 Keith Wrightson and David Levine, *Poverty and piety in an English village: Terling, 1525–1700* (1979).

18 For example, M. K. Ashby, *The changing English village, 1066–1914* [Bledington, Gloucs.] (1974); Dennis Clarke and Anthony Stoyel, *Otford in Kent, a history* (1975).

19 For example, H. M. Colvin, *A history of Deddington, Oxfordshire* (1963), 115 pages plus appendices; A. F. Bottomley, *Short history of Southwold* [Suffolk] (1974), 15 pages.

20 From conversation with the late J. T. Munday, historian of Eriswell and Lakenheath in Suffolk.

21 David Jenkins, *The agricultural community of south-west Wales at the turn of the twentieth century* (1971).

22 Glanmor Williams, *The general and common sort of people, 1540–1640*, University of Exeter (1977), p. 22.

23 *Local Population Studies*, No. 12 (Spring, 1974), 28–33; *Agricultural History Review*, Vol. 19 (1971), Pt II, 156–74.

24 David Dymond, *Writing a church guide*, Church Information Office (1977).

25 J. H. Hexter, *Reappraisals in history* (1961), pp. 194–5.

26 M. Spufford, 'The total history of village communities', *The Local Historian*, Vol. 10, No. 8, 398.

27 Alan Macfarlane, *Reconstructing historical communities* (1977), pp. 42–80.

28  Barry Stapleton, 'Sources for the demographic study of a local community from the sixteenth to the mid-nineteenth century', unpublished report to the SSRC.

29  For the specific challenge of group-work, see V. H. T. Skipp, 'The place of team-work in local history' in Finberg and Skipp, *Local history, objective and pursuit* (1967), pp. 87–102; Alan Rogers (ed.), *Group projects in local history* (1977).

30  As examples of county bibliographies, see *A bibliography of the history and topography of Cumberland and Westmorland,* compiled by Henry W. Hodgson (1968); *The Kent bibliography,* compiled by George Bennett (1977); *A Suffolk bibliography,* compiled by A. V. Steward (1979).

31  As an example, see *Suffolk agriculture: a critical bibliography,* compiled by David Dymond, Clive Paine and Monica Place, Suffolk Record Office (1978).

32  For comparison, see *British Archaeological Abstracts,* published twice a year by the Council for British Archaeology.

33  Published by Phillimore in the series 'History from the sources'.

34  For example, F. H. Erith, *Ardleigh in 1796* (1978). This publishes the detailed census of an Essex parish.

35  See D. M. Barratt and D. G. Vaisey (eds.), *Oxfordshire, a handbook for students of local history* (1973); Alan G. Parker, *Isle of Wight local history: a guide to sources* (1975).

36  R. B. Pugh, *How to write a parish history* (1954), pp. 136–39. It should be noted that the logical order of slips will not necessarily be chronological (see p. 36).

37  The publications of the Record Commissioners contain some interesting flaws. For instance, in the Hundred Rolls of the late thirteenth century (*Rotuli Hundredorum,* Vol. II (1818), p. 499), the name *Okacerif* proves to be a misreading of *Chateris* (Chatteris, Cambs.). The confusions are understandable: between C and O, h and k, t and c, s and f. (I am indebted to Lionel Munby for this reference.)

38  Margaret Spufford, 'The total history of village communities', *The Local Historian,* Vol. 10, No. 8 (Nov. 1973), 400.

39  Michael Turner, 'Recent progress in the study of Parliamentary enclosure', *The Local Historian,* Vol. 12, No. 1, 18–25; Margaret Gelling, 'Recent work on Anglo-Saxon charters', *The Local Historian,* Vol. 13, No. 4, 209–16.

40  L. C. Hector, *Handwriting of English documents* (1958); Giles E. Dawson and Laetitia Kennedy-Skipton, *Elizabethan handwriting, 1500–1650* (1966); Charles Johnson and Hilary Jenkinson, *English court hand, AD 1066–1500* (1915).

41  K. C. Newton, *Medieval local records – a reading aid,* Historical Assoc. (1971); F. G. Emmison, *How to read local archives, 1550–1700* (1967).

42 Everyone who teaches palaeography will remember examples of 'clangers'. My favourite comes from a will of about 1500: the phrase '20 shillings for tithes forgotten (Tythes for ʒetyn)' was rendered as '20 shillings for tips for Satan'.

43 G. Kitson Clark, *The critical historian* (1967), especially sections 8 and 9.

44 D. N. J. MacCulloch (ed.), *The chorography of Suffolk*, Suffolk Records Soc., Vol. XIX (1976).

45 R. Floud, *An introduction to quantitative methods for historians* (1973); Leslie Bradley, *A glossary for local population studies* (2nd ed. 1978), Pt 2 – statistical terms.

46 E. A. Wrigley, 'Family limitation in pre-industrial England', *Economic History Review*, 2nd series, XIX (1966), 82–109.

47 Adrian Henstock, 'House repopulation from the census returns of 1841 and 1851', *Local Population Studies*, No. 10 (Spring 1973), 37–52.

48 See Terence Gwynne and Michael Sell, 'Census enumeration books: a study of mid-nineteenth century immigration', *The Local Historian*, Vol. 12, No. 2, 74–9.

49 Barrie Trinder in Alan Rogers and Trevor Rowley (eds.) *Landscapes and documents* (1974), p. 79. The special problems of co-ordinating archaeology and history are discussed in D. P. Dymond, *Archaeology and history* (1974), sections 4, 5 and 6.

50 H. P. R. Finberg quoting R. H. Worth in Joan Thirsk (ed.), *Agricultural history of England and Wales*, Vol. IV, vii.

51 H. M. Colvin, *A history of Deddington, Oxfordshire* (1963); W. G. Hoskins, *The midland peasant* (1965).

52 G. R. Elton, *The practice of history* (1967), p. 118; Arthur Marwick, *Introduction to History* (Open University, 1977), pp. 113–17.

53 W. G. Hoskins, *Local history in England* (2nd ed. 1972), p. 227.

54 Marc Bloch, *The historian's craft* (1954), p. 43.

55 Alan Rogers, *Approaches to local history* (2nd ed. 1977), pp. 127–8.

56 Lionel Munby in *The Local Historian*, Vol. 13, No. 4 (1978), review, p. 240.

57 H. P. R. Finberg in Finberg and Skipp, *Local history, objective and pursuit* (1967), p. 76.

58 E. P. Thompson, *The making of the English working class*, Pelican (1968), pp. 237–8.

59 H. P. R. Finberg in Finberg and Skipp, *Local history, objective and pursuit* (1967), p. 85.

60 James Batley, 'Publishing local history: a practical approach', *The Local Historian*, Vol. 12, No. 7, 360–64; Vol. 12, No. 8, 424–29; Vol. 13, No. 3, 163–67; Vol. 13, No. 4, 227–32.

# PUBLISHED WORKS

Included in this general category are transcripts, translations, calendars (summaries of original documents), lists and indexes which help us to find relevant documents, and finally the secondary works of historians which reveal the current state of knowledge, opinion and controversy.

## A Transcripts and translations

For a general introduction to these, see E. L. C. Mullins, *Texts and calendars* (Royal Hist. Soc. 1958). He lists the publications of the old Record Commissioners set up in 1800, of the Public Record Office, of national societies (e.g. Camden, Selden and Harleian), and of local record societies (e.g. Surtees, Thoresby and Norfolk).

The text of Domesday Book will be found in translation in the general volumes published for each county by the Victoria County History, and in a new series now being published by Phillimore.

In the nineteenth century the Record Commissioners published transcripts of many important documents with a wide geographical coverage (e.g. the Hundred Rolls of the late thirteenth century, the Ecclesiastical Taxation of 1291, the Inquisition of the Ninth of 1340/1 and the Valor Ecclesiasticus of 1535).

Of the official *Calendars,* a local historian should always be prepared to search through the more obvious series (e.g. the Patent Rolls, Close Rolls, Charter Rolls, Inquisitions Post Mortem, Acts of the Privy Council, and Letters and Papers of the reign of Henry VIII). Such volumes are usually indexed, though not always adequately by modern standards. Another great series of Calendars has been produced by the Historical Manuscripts Commission, analysing the collections of individuals, corporations, dioceses, etc.

It should not be forgotten that individual local historians and antiquaries have published and edited texts, sometimes singly and sometimes in series (e.g. transcripts of parish registers, collections of wills, etc.).

An astonishing amount of material has appeared for generations in the form of *Notes and Queries* or *Miscellanies.* (E.g. *East Anglian Notes and Queries,* 4 vols. edited by S. Tymms 1858–69, 13 vols. New Series 1885–1910; *East Anglian Miscellany* 1901–58).

County historical and archaeological journals also contain many transcripts and translations of original documents, usually embedded in articles.

## B Indexes to original sources

The *Guide to the Public Records,* 2 vols. (1963) gives general guidance on the contents of the Public Record Office, London, at Chancery Lane and Kew (known as PRO). For example it will tell you that lists of church goods taken in the reigns of Edward VI and Mary are to be found under E 117, and that the Corn Returns of 1799 to 1949 are under MAF 10.

More detailed and of great value to the local historian are the *PRO Lists and Indexes* and the parallel productions of the List and Index Society. These give you references to individual documents with brief details of contents, places and personal names. The scores of volumes already printed cover, for example, many manorial documents kept in the PRO (Court rolls, Ministers' Accounts and Surveys), the Proceedings of the Star Chamber, and Special Commissions of the Exchequer.

*Note:* A pamphlet called *Record Publications, Sectional List No. 24* lists all the official published indexes, transcripts and calendars of documents in the national archives. While working through the volumes in a library, it is useful to be able to tick them off on this list.

In some counties, the County Record Office has published guides to sources. Newsletters, lists of accessions and hand-outs are also produced to help the searcher.

At the National Register of Archives, Quality Court, Chancery Lane, London WC2, can be found a register of manorial records.

## C Bibliographies of secondary works

The Historical Association has published several useful lists of books and articles. For example:

*English local history handlist,* edited by F. W. Kuhlicke and F. G. Emmison.

*The history of the church, a select bibliography,* by Owen Chadwick.

*Local history from Blue Books,* by W. R. Powell (This lists some of the more useful sessional papers of Parliament – really these are primary sources).

Regional and county bibliographies are of great value. See for example: *A Bibliography of Norfolk history,* compiled by E. Darroch and B. Taylor (1975).

To keep abreast of new books, the local historian must read reviews in journals such as *History* (published by the Historical Association) and *The Local Historian* (published by the British Association for Local History).

# BASIC RULES FOR TRANSCRIBING DOCUMENTS

(1) The aim is to reproduce the text as accurately as possible: nothing is to be added or omitted without acknowledgement.

(2) Each transcript should be headed with a reference to both repository and document. For example: Public Record Office (*or* PRO), E 179/260/5.

(3) The numbers of pages, folios or membranes should be shown at the appropriate points in the text, in square brackets. For front and back faces of each folio, use r (recto) and v (verso); for the back of a membrane use d (dorso).

(4) To mark the end of each line in the original text, use an oblique stroke /.

(5) Abbreviations which are absolutely clear should be extended in square brackets, for example, *messuag[ium]*. If you have doubts, put either an apostrophe for the part omitted, for example, *messuag'*, or qualify your extension by adding a question mark, for example, *messuag[ium?]*.

(6) Retain the original spelling, however idiosyncratic or inconsistent. Also retain the original punctuation (if it exists), paragraphing, capital letters (however odd their distribution) and old English letters like the 'thorn' (þ) and 'yogh' (ȝ). Do not at this stage add your own punctuation or 'correct' the spelling.

(7) Figures and numerals should be given as in the original (whether Roman, Arabic or a mixture of the two).

(8) Rubrics and marginal headings should be underlined. Paragraph or similar marks should be noted.

(9) Alterations in the manuscript should be accepted, but the original version (if legible) should be given in a footnote or marginal note. Changes of handwriting or ink should be similarly noted.

(10) Gaps, tears and illegible sections should be indicated by square or angle brackets <...>; the approximate length of the missing part can be shown by a line of points within the brackets, or given in a special footnote. Remember that legibility can sometimes be improved by the use of an ultra-violet lamp.

(11) Recurring words and phrases may be represented by initials or some other contraction, but say what has been done in an introductory note. An obvious example from Domesday Book is TRE (*tempore Regis Edwardi*, 'in the time of King Edward').

(12) To show that a mistake is not the transcriber's but appears in the manuscript itself, use [sic] meaning 'thus'.

N.B. When it comes to *editing texts for publication,* a different set of rules is often adopted. For example:

Punctuation is modernised.

Capitalisation is modernised.

Abbreviations are extended, without brackets save in cases of doubt.

Certain letters are modernised (u and v, i and j, c and t).

The ampersand (&) is extended.

See R. F. Hunnisett, *Editing records for publication, Archives and the user, No. 4* (1977).

## Palaeography – a reading list (indispensable books are asterisked)

L. C. Hector, *The handwriting of English documents,* 2nd ed. (1966).

K. C. Newton, *Medieval local records, a reading aid* (Hist. Assoc. 1971).

F. G. Emmison, *How to read local archives* (Hist. Assoc. 1967).

Hilda Grieve, *Examples of English handwriting, 1150–1750* (Essex R.O. 1954 and later).

*C. T. Martin, *The record interpreter* (George Olms, reprint of 1969).

*C. R. Cheney, *Handbook of dates* (Royal Hist. Soc. 1955).

For the specific problem of translation see:

*R. E. Latham, *Revised medieval Latin word-list* (1954).

Eileen A. Gooder, *Latin for local history* (1961).

*Lewis and Short, *Latin dictionary.*

B. H. Kennedy, *The shorter Latin primer.*

# HISTORICAL DATING

## Some exercises

By using C. R. Cheney, *Handbook of dates* (Royal Historical Society, 1955), and the methods described on pp. 21, convert the following into modern-style dates (i.e. the year AD and/or the day of the month):

(1) 18 Edward I
(2) 9 Richard II
(3) 12 Charles II
(4) All Souls' Day
(5) Feast of St Dionysius
(6) Translation of St Thomas the Martyr
(7) Sunday after feast of St Ambrose, 2 Edward II
(8) Wednesday before the Nativity of the B.V.M., 10 Edward III
(9) Thursday after the feast of St Mathias, 5 Henry V.
(10) Monday after the decollation of St John the Baptist, 37 Edward III
(11) 9th January, 1709/10

*(The answers are given on p. 90)*

# ANALYSIS

## A transcript sampled from the lay subsidy of 1524–5

| CRATFIELD (near Halesworth, Suffolk) | [£ | s | d] |
|---|---|---|---|
| The Town box in mone £6:13:4 | – | 3 | 4 |
| John Duke gentleman in landes be yer £20 | – | 1 0 | 0 |
| John Smyth in moveabilles £20 | – | 1 0 | 0 |
| Edmund Brodbank in goodes £20 | – | 1 0 | 0 |
| John Cooke in moveabylles £9 | – | 4 | 6 |
| William Orforth in goodes £10 | – | 5 | 0 |
| John Stulberd in goodes £10 | – | 5 | 0 |
| John Smyth barker in goodes £15 | – | 7 | 6 |
| Thomas Smyth de le Haugh in goodes £8 | – | 4 | 0 |
| John Thurketell in goodes £6 | – | 3 | 0 |
| Thomas Smyth bocher in goodes £5 | – | 2 | 6 |
| Thomas Clamp in goodes £4 | – | 2 | 0 |
| John Smyth de Letyll Haugh in goodes £4 | – | 2 | 0 |
| William Gylberd in goodes £2 | – | 1 | 0 |
| John Smyth of Norwoode in goodes £4 | – | 2 | 0 |
| John Newson in goodes £10 | – | 5 | 0 |
| Laurens Chylderhous in goodes £6 | – | 3 | 0 |
| Nicholas Stulberd in goodes £4 | – | 2 | 0 |
| John Clerk thelder in goodes £6 | – | 3 | 0 |
| John Tye in goodes £4 | – | 2 | 0 |
| John Mychell in goodes £6 | – | 3 | 0 |
| Thomas Pantre in goodes £3 | – | 1 | 6 |
| John Thurketell thelder in goodes £3 | – | 1 | 6 |
| William Ede in goodes £3 | – | 1 | 6 |
| Robert Bemond in goodes £3 | – | 1 | 6 |
| Stephen Fastlyn in landes be yer £2 | – | 2 | 0 |
| John Bateman in goodes £3 | – | 1 | 6 |
| John Sherman in goodes £3 | – | 1 | 6 |
| Robert Botomle in goodes £3 | – | 1 | 6 |
| Richard Brodbank in goodes £4 | – | 2 | 0 |
| John Cordy in goodes £3 | – | 1 | 6 |
| William Pantre in landes be yer £1 | – | 1 | 0 |
| John Rous in landes be yer £1 | – | 1 | 0 |

| | | | |
|---|---|---|---|
| John Clerk the yonger in goodes £2 | – | 1 | 0 |
| John Rous the yonger in goodes £2 | – | 1 | 0 |
| William Cordy in goodes £2 | – | 1 | 0 |
| Thomas Cordy in goodes £2 | – | 1 | 0 |
| Robert Russell in goodes £2 | – | 1 | 0 |
| John Smyth in goodes £2 | – | 1 | 0 |
| Thomas Coker, John Bankys, John Clamp, Edmund Myller, in wages £1 (each) | – | 1 | 4 |
| Margaret Blobell in goodes £4 | – | 2 | 0 |
| Agnes Rous in goodes £3 | – | 1 | 6 |
| Elizabeth Kebell in landes £1 | – | 1 | 0 |
| Isabell Mellys in goodes £3 | – | 1 | 6 |
| Johanne Kebyll in landes be yer £1 | – | 1 | 0 |
| William Mylles in wages £1 | – | | 4 |
| Thomas Bateman in goodes £2 | – | 1 | 0 |
| William Bloboll in goodes £2 | – | 1 | 0 |
| William Ferrour in goodes £2 | – | 1 | 0 |

Summa hujus ville £7  15  6

(from *Suffolk in 1524,* Suffolk Green Book, No. X, (1910), pp. 80–82, taken from PRO: E 179/180/171)

*(See overleaf, p. 56, for ways of analysing this document.)*

# 1524 Lay subsidy – a scheme for analysis

(1) Number of tax-payers in the parish of $x$?
(2) Estimated total population? (A multiplier of 4·5 is often used).
(3) Number of people with social status indicated? Give details.
(4) List occupations given.
(5) How many women? How many widows?
(6) Are any 'addresses' given? Can they be identified on the ground?
(7) List the institutional payments (on town goods, church monies, guilds, etc.)
(8) Total payment made for parish or town.
(9) How many people paid in lands?
(10) How many people paid in goods?
(11) How many people paid in wages?
(12) How many people paid the basic 4d?
(13) Tabulate the payments, to give some indication of social structure.

**Note**

After analysing the returns for a single parish, one can profitably extend the work by comparing the wealth of different parishes, hundreds or counties.

Local surnames can be compared with those given in the Hearth Tax lists. In Norfolk, for example, McKinley found that only 20 per cent of the surnames listed in 1524 were still in the same parishes in 1666.

**Exercise**

Draw up a scheme of analysis for a major source, or a group of sources, with which you are familiar. Test it to see what kind of generalisations emerge.

# FORM PRODUCED BY CAMBRIDGE GROUP FOR ANALYSING BURIALS IN PARISH REGISTERS

## BURIALS

PARISH: COLYTON

County: Devon

YEARS: 1661–80

| YEAR | Jan. | Feb. | Mar. | Apr. | May | June | July | Aug. | Sept. | Oct. | Nov. | Dec. | Civil Year (totals) | Jan-July | Aug-Dec. | Harvest Year (totals) | Wanderers | Comments |
|---|---|---|---|---|---|---|---|---|---|---|---|---|---|---|---|---|---|---|
| 1661 | 0 | 0 | 4 | 3 | 1 | 5 | 8 | 3 | 3 | 2 | 3 | 4 | 36 | 21 | 15 | 33 | | ← |
| 1662 | 2 | 2 | 2 | 3 | 3 | 3 | 3 | 3 | 1 | 6 | 2 | 3 | 33 | 18 | 15 | 34 | | In these two |
| 1663 | 2 | 1 | 7 | 2 | 1 | 2 | 4 | 2 | 0 | 6 | 1 | 2 | 30 | 19 | 11 | 29 | | decades the |
| 1664 | 3 | 1 | 3 | 2 | 2 | 6 | 1 | 3 | 2 | 2 | 3 | 1 | 29 | 18 | 11 | 27 | | register |
| 1665 | 2 | 1 | 2 | 3 | 4 | 3 | 1 | 2 | 4 | 4 | 1 | 2 | 26 | 16 | 10 | 34 | | consistently |
| 1666 | 5 | 4 | 2 | 4 | 4 | 2 | 3 | 1 | 6 | 2 | 1 | 7 | 39 | 24 | 15 | 45 | | uses the |
| 1667 | 4 | 1 | 5 | 6 | 5 | 8 | 1 | 1 | 6 | 5 | 3 | 10 | 55 | 30 | 25 | 53 | | 'full' form |
| 1668 | 2 | 1 | 8 | 8 | 4 | 1 | 4 | 5 | 3 | 1 | 1 | 8 | 46 | 28 | 18 | 53 | | of entry |
| 1669 | 5 | 6 | 9 | 4 | 5 | 3 | 3 | 7 | 6 | 9 | 7 | 6 | 70 | 35 | 35 | 74 | | and is |
| 1670 | 7 | 13 | 3 | 3 | 6 | 2 | 5 | 14 | 20 | 6 | 7 | 9 | 95 | 39 | 56 | 93 | | usable for |
| 1671 | 8 | 4 | 6 | 6 | 3 | 3 | 7 | 7 | 6 | 4 | 2 | 7 | 63 | 37 | 26 | 57 | | reconstitution. |
| 1672 | 8 | 3 | 6 | 2 | 7 | 2 | 3 | 6 | 3 | 3 | 4 | 2 | 49 | 31 | 18 | 29 | | Details of |
| 1673 | 3 | 3 | 0 | 3 | 2 | 0 | 0 | 1 | 1 | 2 | 2 | 7 | 24 | 11 | 13 | 48 | | residence are |
| 1674 | 4 | 4 | 9 | 5 | 7 | 3 | 3 | 0 | 3 | 1 | 2 | 4 | 45 | 35 | 16 | 35 | | often given |
| 1675 | 5 | 3 | 0 | 4 | 5 | 7 | 1 | 4 | 2 | 3 | 2 | 6 | 42 | 25 | 17 | 60 | | but |
| 1676 | 6 | 8 | 6 | 2 | 6 | 10 | 5 | 4 | 7 | 7 | 6 | 6 | 73 | 43 | 30 | 62 | | occupations very |
| 1677 | 5 | 6 | 3 | 3 | 3 | 5 | 7 | 7 | 4 | 0 | 6 | 6 | 55 | 32 | 23 | 61 | | seldom |
| 1678 | 2 | 6 | 7 | 6 | 7 | 1 | 5 | 3 | 4 | 7 | 6 | 7 | 65 | 38 | 27 | 56 | | |
| 1679 | 5 | 1 | 7 | 7 | 6 | 4 | 4 | 2 | 2 | 4 | 4 | 6 | 47 | 29 | 18 | 43 | | → |
| 1680 | 5 | 2 | 7 | 6 | 2 | 4 | 4 | 2 | 4 | 6 | 0 | 4 | 41 | 25 | 16 | 37 | | |
| TOTAL | 83 | 70 | 93 | 82 | 81 | 75 | 70 | 77 | 82 | 80 | 63 | 107 | 963 | 554 | 409 | 963 | | |

[from E. A. Wrigley (ed.) *An introduction to English historical demography* (1966), p. 113]

57

# FORM OF ANALYSIS FOR INDIVIDUAL PROBATE INVENTORIES, DESIGNED BY RACHEL GARRARD

| Name | Occupation | Date | Place | Total | Notes, will | Appraisers | Ref |
|---|---|---|---|---|---|---|---|
| John How | (yeo) | 24 July 1685 | Bradfield St Clare | 91-13-10 | Goodwin 189 | John Steame, Charles Steame, John Spurgon | 1C500/3/22(55) |

| Room . . . | Sleeping | Seating | Tables | Storage, Display | Fire | Fittings | (Cooking) Utensils | Hangings, Textiles | Linen | Plate . . . | Light, Miscell |
|---|---|---|---|---|---|---|---|---|---|---|---|
| Hall | | 2 forms, 2 jst — 6 C. | 2 T. £1 | liv. c'6 | jack, 2 bnd spits, 2 trammels, 1 bar, 1 pitch, pr cobi, fp, tongs, bellows | | warming pan | 4 cushns. £1 | | | gun, pr. bandileers, sml. things 1.10.0 |
| Parlour | fb, b/s, things belong fb, tb/s, fb, things belonging £10.10.0 | | | 2 hutches, 2 boxes, glass keep 13/4 | | | | | 10 pr. sh, 4 pr. pillows, 2 Tcl, doz n'k, other linen £2 | | |
| Hall Chamber | | | | | | | pan, bu, riddle, shovel 6/- | | | | peel wheat £5 |
| Plr Chamber | | | | | | | | | | | |
| the Chamber | 2 s, bfs, all things belonging £4 | | | a trunk | | | pr. scales & weights | | | | sml. things in room 5/-; peel. wool 15/- |
| | | | | | | | | | | | |
| | | | | | | | | | | | |
| Dairy + dairy chamber | | | | | | | dairy vessels £1 | | | | butter, cheese £5 |
| Buttery | | | | | | | 4 beer vessels, drip pan, other small things 15/- | | | brass + pewter £3 | |
| Backhouse | | | | | | | sml. copper, brewing tubs, kneading trough, small things £2 | | | | |
| | | | | | | | | | | | |

| | | | |
|---|---|---|---|
| Domestic Industry | | | |
| Clothes | wearing apparel } £4 | | |
| Cash | money in purse at death } | Debt | Investment |
| Livestock Grain | hay + grass in barn + to make £5; 10 sheep. 14 lambs £4; 4 milk cows £12; 2 sml. hogs £1. 10. 0; 2 mares, a 2yr old colt £8; 2½ ac. wheat 6-5-0; 3 roods bly. 1-10-0; 4 ac peas + bullimong. 6-0-0 | | 4 ac summerland + rent of land 2-0-0 |
| Husbandry | mill house – a horsemill 1-10-0; a cart, tumbrils, pr harrows, swathe rake £2; 4 a. collers, 3 pr ploughtraces, cartsaddle, shovel, pr a. tilbells, [illegible], forks, rakes, spade, mattock, lumber 1-2-6 | | |
| Shop Trade | | | |
| N.B.s | | | |

[from Rachel P. Garrard 'English probate inventories and their use in studying the significance of the domestic interior, 1570–1700' in *AAG Bijdragen*, 23 (1980), p. 78]

# FORM FOR ASSEMBLING INFORMATION FROM DIFFERENT SOURCES, DESIGNED BY ROGER FIELDHOUSE

Each form relates to a single person; it is based on the relevant will and inventory, and draws on returns for a lay subsidy and hearth-tax. Forms of this general type could also carry information from parish registers, court rolls, poor-law records, etc.

| | | |
|---|---|---|
| NAME *Peter Bukton* | Date of will/inv. | 15 *March* 1674 <br> 10 *June* 1675 |
| 1544 Lay Sub. assessment | — | 1673 Hearth Tax: No. of hearths | 6 *hearths* |

**Occupation(s)** *Cordiner*

**Family** Wife *Jane* — Mother *(Anne Bukton)* Sons: *Matthew, William, Peter* Daughters: *Margaret, Anne*

**Details of house(s)** in *Freuchgate* (7 rooms + shop)
*Forehouse    Back Chamber    Further Chamber*
*Kitchen    Chamber over House    Shop.*
*Parlour    Chamber over Shop*

**Land/other property** 2 *burgages* in *Freuchgate    Jolly Close*
2 *acres of arable* in *Low East Field    Pickering House (Freuch gate)*
*Acre of arable* in *Low East Field*
*Close of meadow* in *High East Field    Close near St. Nicholas*

**Bequests (other than listed above)**
£60 *each to his 2 dtrs., Margaret and Anne*

**Cash (Inv.).** £13. 6. 8.

**Farm or trade stock/tools etc. (Itemise interesting details)**

*Leather* £17. 0. 0. ⎫   1 *horse* 4. 10. 0 ⎫
*Shoes* £18. 10. 2. ⎬ £56. 10. 2   2 *cows* 8. 0. 0. ⎬ £20
*Farm stock* £21. 0. 0. ⎭   *Corn* 7. 10. 0. ⎭

**Household goods, furniture, etc. (Itemise interesting details)**

*Furniture etc.* £19. 6. 8. ⟶ *includes*:
*Silver + pewter* 6. 0. 0.   1 *glass case*
*Brass* 2. 5. 0.   2 *standing beds with curtain valances and patter beds*
  1 *seeing glass*
  *linen*

**Total value of inv.** £225. 7. 7. (*excluding credits*)

**Credit** £140. 2. 5     **Debts** £10. 3. 4.

**Other information**
*Shoes in this inventory were valued as follows:*
*mens 3/- ; boys 1/6 ; boots 5/-*
*womens 2/- ; childrens 10ᵈ.*

[from Alan Rogers (ed.) *Group projects in local history* (1977), p. 79]

59

# THE HISTORIAN AND HIS SOURCES

**A.** An historian does not normally summarise each document's strengths and weaknesses in his writing. That would be tedious, and could be an excuse for not attempting to write at a higher, more creative level. If, however, a document (or group of documents) is of really central importance in his work, and poses interesting problems of interpretation, the historian can with effect include a deliberate assessment. For example:

T. S. Willan, *An eighteenth-century shopkeeper: Abraham Dent of Kirkby Stephen* (1970), p. 9:
'Among the records relating to the shop is a day book in which were entered goods sold, but not paid for at the time of sale. When the goods were finally paid for, the entry was crossed through. These entries of credit sales give the quantity and price of the goods and the customer's name. They extend from May 1762 to September 1765, though there are a few entries of later date. Obviously these credit sales do not give a complete picture of the trade during those years, but they do give a very detailed picture of what was sold in the shop and to whom. They show clearly that the Dents were grocers, mercers and stationers, though it is interesting to note that they were never described as grocers or stationers, which shows the limitations of contemporary descriptions. Most of the goods sold in the shop could be loosely classified as grocery, mercery and stationery.'

*Note:* some writers in polishing their final draft might have dropped the last sentence as superfluous.

**B.** If the historian is in luck, he will find sources which are complementary in the information they give. In other words, the weaknesses of one group of documents may be balanced by the strengths of another. Indeed, whenever the historian uses two or more documents which are relevant to his subject, he will find information which is, to some extent, complementary. Though problems of interpretation always arise, this kind of cross-fertilisation enables him to build up a more detailed, and therefore more truthful, picture of the past.

Alan Macfarlane, *Witchcraft in Tudor and Stuart England* (1970), p. 24:
'There were over 500 indictments for witchcraft at the Essex Assizes. A typical one will show the nature of prosecutions at this court. At the Essex

Hilary Sessions in 1579, Ellen Smyth of Maldon, spinster, was accused of bewitching Susan Webbe, aged about four years. The bewitching was said to have occurred on 7 March 1579 and the child to have died at Maldon on the 8th. The presentment was found to be a "true bill" by the Grand Jury and the defendant was found guilty and judged according to the Statute. It will be immediately seen that such indictments provide information on a number of problems: the place of residence, age, sex, and marital position of witch and victim; the duration and nature of the bewitching; the verdict of the two jurors. Nevertheless, it is important to remember that indictments only give a summary of the outline of the prosecutions. The examinations and evidence at the Assize are omitted.† The occasional contemporary account of an Assize trial preserved in a witchcraft pamphlet corrects the distorted effect of such indictments. Ellen Smyth's case is among those described at greater length in a pamphlet. We learn that Ellen was the daughter of Alice Chaundeler, previously executed for witchcraft; that Ellen quarrelled with her stepfather over an inheritance and that he subsequently became ill; that she was believed to own a toad familiar which, when burnt, caused its mistress pain; that her child-victim's mother was sent mad by the sight of another familiar like a black dog; that Ellen's son described his mother's three spirits called "greate Dicke", "little Dicke", and "Willet", and that the bottles and wool-pack in which they were supposedly housed were discovered after a search of her house. Thus we see that the evidence written down in the Assize and Quarter Sessions records is only the barest outline of a mass of beliefs and suspicions.'

*Note:* †It might have been worthwhile beginning a new paragraph at this point, to emphasise the new source.

**C.** This third extract shows the difficulties which we face in trying to build up an interpretation from two or more sources. Often documents are not dealing with exactly the same categories. Thus although a lay subsidy and a court roll may deal with the same historical persons, the first refers to them as taxable individuals and the second as manorial tenants and offenders. Unless the historian appreciates such differences, and allows for them, he cannot see the implications which each document has for the others, and he therefore cannot relate and interlock his evidence to form an acceptable interpretation. Here we see an historian wrestling grimly with difficult sources, but on this occasion not winning too convincingly!

Margaret Spufford, *Contrasting communities* (1974), p. 23:
    'Detailed examination of the evidence available on the size of Orwell shows just how misleading subsidy returns can be. There were fifty-two

taxable individuals there in 1524, and forty-six households, according to the bishop, in 1563. This difference is probably accounted for by the changed basis of assessment, rather than by any real change. Only forty-five houses were recorded by the hearth tax assessors of 1664, however. This was certainly an underestimate, for the names of all the tenants of the manor, both freeholders and copyholders, were listed in 1649, 1650 and 1672. The numbers recorded were both fairly consistent and static, between fifty-four in 1650 and fifty in 1670. The map made in the 1670s shows fifty-five houses. There may therefore have been an increase of about a fifth in the number of households between the bishop's estimate in 1563, and the 1670s, always provided that the bishop's figure was accurate. The baptism trends from the parish registers suggest fewer families in Orwell in the 1660s than in the 1570s. However, despite the proven inaccuracy of the hearth tax in this instance, the picture of the overall size of Orwell remains a fairly static one with its fifty-two taxable adults in the 1520s, and its fifty to fifty-four tenants in the 1670s.'

# THE ORGANISATION OF A PIECE OF HISTORICAL WRITING – I

D. M. Palliser's study of 'Dearth and disease in Staffordshire, 1540–1670' is one of twelve essays written in honour of W. G. Hoskins, and published in 1974 under the title *Rural change and urban growth, 1500–1800* (edited by C. W. Chalklin and M. A. Havinden). It is an impressive piece of professional history, readable and stimulating. A mass of detail and statistics is given shape by the writer's determination to interpret and, where possible, to draw conclusions.

The following notes present in a simplified form the structure of ideas and questions which lies inside the essay, that is, the deliberate design which should lie inside any piece of historical writing.

## The overall design
Dr Palliser's article contains several sections of varying length, planned roughly as follows:
A brief introduction to demography and related subjects.
A statement of the purpose of the article, with its geographical and chronological limits.
A chronological survey in considerable detail, giving the evidence for dearth and disease. This forms the bulk of the study.
Some general points about epidemics.
The identification of two kinds of general mortality, afflicting both towns and countryside.
Three detailed examples, showing the trends of disease and dearth.

## The detailed argument
Each of these sections is now analysed to show how the argument is unfolded in detail by the writer. [Occasional comments and criticisms are inserted within square brackets.]

**Introduction:** demographic history recently stimulated by the Cambridge Group; a wide range of sources are now exploited, which previously had only been used by genealogists. Related subjects are also advancing: the history of climate, of disease, also the chronology of harvests and famines.

**Purpose:** the article is designed to chart the 'chronology of crisis' in Staffordshire, using the surviving parish registers, from 1538 when they were begun until the disappearance of bubonic plague *c*. 1670.
No systematic records of prices exist for Staffordshire. National figures therefore have to be used, based largely on southern sources.

**Geographical:** the county of Staffordshire straddles the boundary between the lowland and highland zones: two uplands with poor soils divided by the richer plain of the Trent. Thinly peopled with a few towns.

**Demographic background:** before 1538 the demographic history of Staffordshire is obscure. The Black Death of 1349 had clearly caused devastation, but not as much as in other counties. Little documentary evidence exists for the late fourteenth and the fifteenth centuries, but the contraction of settlement was widespread: at least eighteen villages and hamlets disappeared between the 1320s and 1530s.

**Chronological survey for sixteenth and seventeenth centuries:** the first epidemic visible in the registers of Staffordshire occurs in 1551: The Great Sweat, a national phenomenon.
An even worse nationwide epidemic in 1557–9: perhaps a form of influenza preceded by two bad harvests, so perhaps malnutrition was a factor in the spread of disease. Many Staffordshire parishes were affected.
Lengthy gaps in parish registers at this time: a sign of the seriousness of the epidemic. This coincides with the comments of muster commissioners about great mortality.
Then came sixteen harvests in a row, of average quality or above. The county was free of general epidemics, but outbreaks occurred in towns (e.g. Tamworth 1563–5).
1579: a widespread urban epidemic.
1587–8: again high mortality, but no mention of plague; there could be a connection with poor harvests in 1585–6.
1593: the towns were struck again, especially Newcastle, Stafford and Lichfield.
1596–8: another general crisis, the first epidemic to hit rural areas since the 1550s; also a clear connection with below-average harvests during the years 1594–7; huge rise in grain prices.
1603–5: a return to the pattern of urban plague.
Thereafter for nearly forty years, there were few serious epidemics and those almost entirely urban. However, dearths are noticeable: burials of wanderers and destitute recorded in registers.
By contrast the 1640s saw the worst epidemics since 1603–5, chiefly in the

towns. The next twenty years were relatively healthy, apart from scattered outbreaks.

[When dealing with close repetitive details of this kind, the historian must be careful to present them as part of a strong, clear argument. Dr Palliser certainly does this, and frequently inserts sentences which show the general significance of his detail, for example: 'The 1640s, by contrast, saw the worst epidemics in the county since the series of 1603–5'.]

**General points about epidemics:** the seventeenth century was a great divide in English pathological history: bubonic and pneumonic plague disappeared after 1666; other killing diseases became prominent, like small pox and measles. In the sixteenth and seventeenth centuries, 'plague' was an omnibus term which was used for other diseases than bubonic plague itself. So-called plagues were generally urban, and rarely lasted more than a year. The famous outbreak in 1665 at the village of Eyam in Derbyshire was a striking exception to the rule.

**Two kinds of general mortality:** this is mortality which affects town and country alike. It falls into two categories:
(1) periodic dearths arising from harvest failures; less lethal than 'plagues' but could run on for years – especially dangerous if they coincided with the arrival of disease.
(2) epidemics which were, at the time, distinguished from plague (e.g. the 'sweating sickness' of 1551 and the 'new sickness' of 1557–9). These virus diseases, especially when they coincided with malnutrition, were lethal.

**Identifying diseases:** the identification of actual diseases is difficult, but urban 'plagues' in the summer months were probably bubonic. Bubonic plague disappears c. 1670. Reasons? Black rat replaced by brown? The effects of the Great Rebuilding?

[This last paragraph seems rather isolated: its contents might have been better assimilated into the earlier discussion of epidemics.]

**Three detailed examples:** showing the trends of disease and dearth in terms of deaths, marriages and conceptions. (Three graphs)
(1) Tamworth, 1579 – epidemic of plague with summer peak.
(2) Newcastle, 1593 – epidemic with winter peak.
(3) Tamworth, 1596–8 – famine and dearth, associated with dysentery. Mortality reaches a climax three to six months after a bad harvest; a succession of winter peaks, each more severe than the last – until a good harvest occurred to break the cycle.

[The peak so soon after harvest is not explained. Why did not the worst mortality occur in the spring or early summer? Did relief schemes, such as the importing of 'foreign' grain, have any effect?]

The graphs also confirm that when burials climbed to a peak, marriages and conceptions fell away. When the crisis passed, the three movements were reversed. 'Scissor' effect. Weddings were more obviously disrupted during short, severe epidemics than in long drawn-out famines. Conceptions fell because of the death of fertile people, and because of the lowered fertility of survivors.

[This is the most original part of the article, which offers ideas of wide application. Dr Palliser identifies significant details and trends within parish registers, and suggests how they may be interpreted. Here we see local evidence being made to contribute powerfully to national history.]

The loss of life was usually repaired by a sharp rise in births; this would subsequently distort the age-structure of the population. The normal situation in both the sixteenth and seventeenth centuries was a surplus of baptisms. Staffordshire's population grew quicker than England's as a whole. Was the growth of population connected with the growth of industry? Which was cause and which effect?

The article concludes with a helpful series of references, often with extra notes and comments.

[Dr Palliser's article talks mainly about 'burials' and 'mortality', and there are few references to individuals or families. However, some contemporary quotations are used to give a more human touch, for example: 'Edward Smith, a poore child dying in the church porch'. A similar article on Devon by W. G. Hoskins provides an interesting comparison: it is probably less penetrating as a piece of research, but distinctly more humane in its style (*Old Devon* (1971), pp. 135–53).]

N.B. This analysis of the content and logic of a published piece is essentially similar to the 'sketch' which writers are recommended to produce as a preliminary to writing (see p. 32).

# THE ORGANISATION OF A PIECE OF HISTORICAL WRITING – II

A good example of parish history is *Otford in Kent: a history* by Dennis Clarke and Anthony Stoyel (1975). Whereas Example I was the work of a full-time professional historian, this book was written by a school-teacher and a retired businessman, largely for local consumption. It amply demonstrates that no essential difference exists between the work of professionals and amateurs. Good history can be written by both groups, and so can bad. Clarke and Stoyel have written an illuminating account of one parish, and have related it to the background of regional and national history. In so doing, they have made sense of local events and ensured that they can be read with profit and enjoyment by local residents *and* outsiders. If all local history were approached in this way, it would undoubtedly cause – to a far greater degree than is now the case – the drastic revision and rewriting of national history.

This sample consists of the first seventeen pages of Chapter 9, which is entitled 'Late-Georgian and Early-Victorian'. It reminds us of the opportunities presented to local historians by the nineteenth century. As in Example I, the following notes attempt to lay bare the succession of ideas within this piece of writing; they identify the main sections, but not necessarily individual paragraphs. The argument is not so tightly constructed and analytical as the first example, but proceeds as a steady chronological narrative. The writing is improved by reference to other parishes in the area, by also indicating the differences between the main village and a hamlet in the same parish, and by the detailed analysis of major sources.

[Occasional comments and criticisms are given in square brackets.]

(1) The chapter begins with mention of the local artist Samuel Palmer and his friends; an idyll of enchanted and privileged youth. Yet the countryside which Palmer painted so romantically was simmering with discontent.
[This is an excellent opening, built around the contrast between young artists and an unhappy labouring population.]

(2) Bad harvests 1828–9, followed by the severe winter of 1829–30. The usual low wages, coupled with more than usual unemployment. In the background was the general election of 1830; reports in the press of barricades and street-fighting in Paris.
[This is a salutary reminder of the outside world.]

(3) Outbreak of the labourers' revolt, smashing threshing machines, burning stacks and farm buildings. Local cases at Orpington, Sevenoaks and Otford itself. Small masters were affected as well as large.

(4) Farmers of the Sevenoaks district reacted by establishing an association for the detection of incendiaries. The first 'Swing Letters' to be delivered in England originated in this district. One recipient was Peter Nouaille, who had inherited a textile mill, and owned a large estate partly in Otford. Some people, like Samuel Palmer, believed that the local labourers were not capable of violence, and blamed outside agitators.

(5) Otford poor-law records survive from 1818. For example in 1828, the chief ratepayers were seven farmers who tenanted and farmed 2,000 of Otford's 2,771 acres: four of them had over 300 acres; the other three between 100 and 200 acres. After them came smaller farmers and tradesmen. All these men were principal members of a select vestry which managed the affairs of the parish. Lower in the social scale were other ratepayers – various smallholders, shopkeepers and artisans. But three out of four adult males were poor labourers or cottagers.

(6) Thirty-six resident ratepayers and forty-three cottagers were not assessed in 1819. Later the status of ratepayer was extended to all but the very poorest – a crushing levy in view of contemporary wages and rents.

(7) 1821 was a peak year: £1,040 spent on poor-relief. Much lower expenditure in the later 1820s: F. R. J. Pateman suggests that the parish was administered more efficiently at this time; in any case, conditions probably improved.
[This analysis of poor-law records shows a creative approach that is so often lacking in parochial studies. The records are used, and not simply quoted.]

(8) Economic conditions are reflected in the rise and fall of local burials: high 1820–24, decreasing 1825–28, a peak in 1831.
[Here a parallel source is thoughtfully invoked.]

(9) From 1826, vestry minute books record applications for relief. 1826–30, an average of 228 applications per annum; 70 per cent were granted, in money, clothing, housing, rents, jobs, food, etc. (They include grants of gin, handkerchiefs and a new wooden leg. The vestry seemed generally sympathetic though it had to cope with some difficult customers.)
[Again, a local source has been 'squeezed': a good balance is achieved between generalisation and colourful detail.]

(10) National public opinion was moving towards a more centralised and harsher system. Hence the Poor Law Amendment Act, 1834.

(11) Otford was in Sevenoaks Union; union workhouse in Sevenoaks, at first laxly administered, then more strictly. Otford's rate burden was much reduced.

(12) Slump of 1837–42. Unusual number of burials at Otford. From 1838–48 the vestry bought coal to resell at reduced price to poor (except to those who kept a dog, and were, presumably, potential poachers). The coal-lists show the number of families in receipt: particularly large in 1847–48, and mainly in Otford village rather than Dunton Green.

(13) Pateman suggested that the Anglican clergy neglected Otford, and that Methodism was gaining strength. But the response to Methodism was not significant until the 1870s.
[This paragraph seems rather out of place, and the point about clerical neglect is not developed.]

(14) The significance of the Tithe Commutation Act, 1836. Otford's tithe award and map of 1844 give the 'first modern survey of the parish'. Seven landlords owned nine-tenths of the parish, which they let to nine farmers. About twelve smaller tenants held from six to seventy-seven acres each: there were also mills, brickworks and limeworks. (A map shows the layout of the nine major farms.)

(15) Although farmers continued to dominate the select vestry, some landlords also contributed to local affairs. For example, John Wreford bought land in 1830, built Broughton House and erected a National School.
[Here the writers have veered off their analysis of the tithe award, which could have been deeper. For example, nothing is said about land-use, the sizes of fields or the numbers of cottage-rows and tenements.]

(16) The three censuses of 1851–71. Growth in the size of the larger farms; some of the smaller farms were absorbed. New kilns, oast-houses and stowages were being built until late in the century. The growing of hops cushioned this area from the worst effects of the depression.

(17) The 'hunting tower' on Otford Mount symbolises the prosperous years of Victorian farming; built by Richard Russell who was a great foxhunter and laid out a steeplechase course on his land. In 1870 Russell became a member of the Highway Board, and supported the parish's attempt to revive the old system of parochial responsibility.
[In the last two sections, the writing deteriorates. Is this, I wonder, the result of having two authors and stitching together two sets of contributions? The drive and direction which are so evident in the earlier part of the chapter have disappeared; no sense of planned argument comes through, and the facts have become rather miscellaneous. We wander inconsequentially from the tower to the Highway Board, and the paragraphs are not properly linked.]

(18) In the later 1860s, real wages began to improve. The average wage for farm labourers in Kent was then 11/8d. No local data are available.

(19) The censuses are analysed, giving the rise and fall of local population and the proportion of farm labourers. Dunton Green in 1861 had fewer farm

labourers, craftsmen and servants than in 1851; in Otford village the trends were reversed. The rise in the number of schoolchildren 1851–61 reflects the scarcity of employment rather than improved educational facilities. A considerable number of people migrated or emigrated. Of 104 males in 1851 in age-group 10–19, seventy-two had left by 1861. Of seventy-six females in 1851 in age-group 10–19, only four had settled in the parish in 1861. Yet during this decade, the natural excess of baptisms over burials had been 106. [This is a highly revealing piece of analysis, based on the comparison of two censuses.]

(20) The growth of Dunton Green. In 1836 twelve stage-coaches passed through on London–Hastings road, and numerous carriers' waggons. A new road over Polhill was constructed in 1834–38. By 1851 Dunton Green had seventeen persons engaged in trade and twenty-seven craftsmen (Otford village had five and eighteen respectively). The population of Dunton Green consisted of four times as many 'foreigners' as natives. A ramshackle, new settlement: from ten houses in 1807 to ninety-seven in 1851. Marriages between Otford and Dunton Green 'were extremely rare'.

(21) Shab Hall, Dunton Green, is the only thatched building left in parish: in 1851 it sheltered six families totalling eighteen people; in 1861 it contained six families totalling thirty people. The presence of two lodgers in 1861 underlines shortage of accommodation.

[Here we are back to an argued analysis of the evidence, but the writers tend to slip in too many facts and figures, not always related to the preceding part of the text.]

(22) Dunton Green's lodging houses: e.g. in 1851 John Barrett had eleven lodgers – six single males, a married couple and three Irish servant girls described as 'visitors'. In 1861 William Carrol had fifteen lodgers.

(23) The reasons for regional depression in 1850s are not satisfactorily established. The loss of the coach trade must be a factor. The parish was revivified after 1861 by the coming of the railways.

(24) In the period 1861–71, the population of the parish increased 40 per cent. Two brickfields were established, and two railway stations.

[The chapter ends with a discussion of the building of the railway, the restoration of the parish church and the evidence for church attendance.]

Appendix 7

# EXAMPLES OF WRITING, WITH DETAILED CRITIQUE – I

The following extract is taken from a local history published in 1933. It contains elementary mistakes which are still committed with monotonous regularity. In fact such seriously flawed writing is now more common than ever, because of the increasing popularity of local history and the flood of modern publications.

To put the case bluntly, this writing is no more than an uncritical rag-bag of facts and anecdotes, very often in the shape of overlong quotations. Even though the author consulted local and national sources, and probably read some general books, he made no attempt to use, shape, or interpret his information. *It is no good quoting an historical fact unless one explains, or debates, its significance.*

This boring, shapeless piece of prose is of little interest – even to a local resident. Yet such writing is frequently justified by authors and publishers on the grounds that it is designed for local consumption, and not for 'academics'. This insults the intelligence of local people, who need properly constructed history as much as anyone else. But let it not be thought that this 'descriptive' or heaping approach to the past is confined to the work of so-called amateurs: it is also a marked feature of many postgraduate theses and can often be found in professional journals.

[At the end of each paragraph, within square brackets, more detailed comments have been inserted.]

'The parish constable was elected annually, and occasionally a headborough was mentioned in the accounts. The first direct reference to a parish beadle appears in the Minutes of 17th November, 1770, when John Wicksteed was appointed at a salary of four pounds a year, "time and expenses being extra".'
[What did the parish constable do? What is the significance of the headborough? We are not told. If it is important for us to know that Mr Wicksteed was paid £4 a year, why is this so? Was it a good or bad wage by contemporary standards?]

'The making of rates was not a popular task, as Mr John Fassett, overseer, found when he called a vestry meeting on 21st May, 1771. No one attended, and so no business could be done. It was not at all a bad way of doing without rates. But the money was wanted sadly,

71

and so after waiting two hours, Mr Fassett called upon his brother overseers and churchwardens, and they took the law into their own hands, and levied a rate of one shilling in the pound – twopence for the Church and tenpence for the poor.'

[The apathy of the vestry is quite an interesting fact, but again nothing is questioned or explained. Why did the vestry have this attitude, and was it usual? How much money was raised by this rate, and how was it actually spent? Does expenditure vary over the years?]

'The churchwarden and constable were the only persons present at a vestry held 23rd September, 1771, and they nominated ten gentlemen as parish surveyors, including the parson, under a penalty of one guinea each if they refused.'

[To appoint as many as ten surveyors of the highways is not usual. And is it true that they were all 'gentlemen'? A succession of particularly short paragraphs is often a sign of weak writing; the same can be said of long rambling paragraphs and the overuse of capital letters!]

'At a vestry held at the Gymcrack, April 21st, 1772, six persons attending, it was ordered "That Mr Harradine pay five shillings for a vestry held June 6th, 1771, six shillings for a vestry held September 23rd, 1771, ditto December 5th, 1771, fourteen shillings and threepence, and for this Easter Vestry One Pound three shillings and threepence halfpenny, making in the whole Four Orders £2. 8s. 6½d".'

[What a boring question! What does it amount to? Was Mr Harradine paying this money for non-payment of rates, or for some other reason?]

'In an act of Parliament, passed in the reign of William III, "for supplying some Defects in the Laws for the Relief of the Poor of this Kindgom," was made the following enactment: "And to the end that the money was raised only for the relief of such as are as well impotent as poor, may not be misapplied and consumed by the idle, sturdy and disorderly beggars: Be it further enacted by the authority aforesaid . . .'

[The quotation continues for another 250 words, and is far too long. The whole extract could have been neatly paraphrased, with perhaps a short and really effective quotation from the original.]

'This Act seems to have been a dead letter in [Ambridge] in this respect, for it was not put into operation until the vestry of 21st April, 1772, when the following was entered on the Minutes: – "It is agreed by this vestry that whoever receives any almens or pencion from this parish shall wear a badge on his or her right sleeve with a P cut in red or blue cloth and two letters for the name of the parish according to an Act of Parliament. Past *neme con*".'

[It is an interesting fact that the 1697 Act was still being invoked late in the eighteenth century. Was there any particular reason? We are clearly meant to be amazed by the quaint spelling.]

# EXAMPLES OF WRITING, WITH DETAILED CRITIQUE – II

This paragraph is taken from the work of a distinguished historical geographer. After each sentence is a comment, in square brackets.

'In some localities, plague and other diseases reversed the general population trend; at Crediton, in Devon, 551 people died during 1571.'
[We start with a generalisation, no doubt based on several known examples, which tells us what the whole paragraph is about. Then we get a particular example from Crediton: this is a statistic which had to be worked out, by somebody, from 551 different entries in the parish register. It is not the kind of fact which simply had to be read in a source and copied. Some writers would have accorded this example the dignity of a separate sentence.]

'The average number of burials for preceding normal years was 40 to 45, so that nearly 500 people must have died of plague in one year in this small town – possibly a third of its population.'
[This sentence starts with a comparison, an invaluable device for showing the significance of an historical fact; it continues with more statistical calculation based on the parish register. Notice how the number 500, though impressive enough, is made even more effective by putting it in a different way, as a proportion of the total population.]

'Between the autumn of 1590 and that of 1592 another 535 also died here.'
[A single and effective statement, which is again the end-product of detailed work on the parish register.]

'Thus Crediton lost over 1,000 people by pestilence in the space of 21 years.'
[Here the writer has drawn together two earlier calculations, and fused them into a more striking generalisation.]

'During the later Middle Ages, plague occurred intermittently, but with a generally decreasing vehemence nationally, and it became increasingly a regional, particularly an urban (especially a London), phenomenon.'

[We are now back to higher generalisation, as at the beginning of the paragraph. This can be a good way of raising ideas which link to the next paragraph or section. As a piece of writing, however, this sentence is bad. It is full of subordinate clauses, adverbs and commas because the writer has tried to put too many complicated ideas into a single sentence. Try to re-write this snippet for yourself; it merits at least two, possibly three, separate sentences.]

**Exercise:** Do a similar analysis for any other paragraph of your choice. What was the author's train of thought, and how effectively did he express it?

# SHORT EXTRACTS OF WRITTEN HISTORY

The following are all genuine quotations from various kinds of historical writing, but for diplomatic reasons names and references are not given. If you had made these statements in a first draft, would you be satisfied? Please comment on these extracts, and if you feel so inclined, re-write them. Not all are bad! My own personal reactions are sometimes given in brackets after the quotation. Standards-wise it is to be hoped that this quotation series may have an ongoing benefit effect on the history writing situation.

(1) 'In Scotland considerable emphasis was placed in the eighteenth-century land division proceedings on the equality of portions within individual sectors. . . .'
[An ungainly, badly constructed sentence with the usual lumping together of nouns.]

(2) 'Concerning the degree of importance of the reduction in smallpox mortality in the general growth of population due to innoculation, my position has changed. . . .'
[When a clause contains more than two or three prepositions, we are in trouble. It usually means that abstract nouns have been overdone, and that we are 'rambling'.]

(3) 'The Saxon huts appear as a new, alien house type, replacing the round houses of the previous millenium, of which 100 sites have now been excavated.'

(4) 'By the system of appropriation the tithes of the parish appropriated belonged to the appropriator.'

(5) 'There is another Hervey de Stanton. I have been trying for some time to bring him in, but could not find a place for him. He comes in now just as the door is being shut. In another minute he would be too late. . . .'

(6) 'I have, therefore, ventured on a new departure in topography, and that is to print and index all my material first, just as it comes to hand; and then hope to begin to write my history under parishes.'
[Recipe for disaster?]

(7) 'To say that Essex was unaffected by the Industrial Revolution is like saying that it was not involved in the Great War.'

(8) '.... 350 miles of canal were used for freight transport purposes.'
[The last two words are totally unnecessary.]

(9) 'The most common form of input medium for a computer is the punched card.'
[Incipient gobbledegook: 'form' and 'medium' are repetitious.]

(10) 'On the other hand, the occupancy structure of Upland farmers was quite different for the size distribution has a strong positive skew.'

(11) 'This book argues that the agricultural revolution took place in England in the sixteenth and seventeenth centuries and not in the eighteenth and nineteenth centuries.'
[A direct and memorable opening to an important book.]

(12) 'Their eligibility for burial in Long Barrows is suggested to have been a function of when they happened to die.'
[Inelegance and jargon are also common in contemporary archaeology.]

(13) 'They [stately homes] reflected the consumption standards and money-spending tendencies of these men.'
[This was written by an Englishman who has done time in the USA. Observe how the important ideas of 'consuming' and 'spending' are emasculated by the abstract nouns, 'standards' and 'tendencies'.]

(14) 'The story suffers under the disadvantage of being untrue.'
[How welcome is a touch of dry humour.]

(15) 'By this means every source reference to a property comes together.'

(16) 'The rooms were usually in line: 'L' shaped houses were rare since watertight roof valleys present problems best avoided.'
[In this and the last example, the logic is flawed.]

(17) 'The project directors are striving to develop student enrichment values.'
[My favourite, which came from California.]

(18) 'Employment and place of origin data was readily available.'
[Notice the effect of that evil little word 'data'. As usual it is assumed to be singular.]

(19) 'While the earth was still settling over St Dominic's bones, the order which he had founded spread with great speed through western Europe.'

(20) 'In order to interpret the Rising effectively it is necessary to consider it in the light of a dysfunctional inter-relationship between, on the one hand, values and ideas, and material factors on the other; the dialectical relationship between substructure and base.'
[How sad that pretentious gibberish of this kind is meant seriously, both as analysis and communication. Note the imbalance of the first clause and the illiteracy of the second.]

(21) 'The specifics of the marital replacement ratio methodologies and other particulars about marriage and the wills will be discussed in detail, below.'
[This is a masterpiece of obscure verbosity. Consider the repetition involved in the use of the three words 'specifics', 'particulars' and 'detail'. Did the writer give a thought to the effect of '. . . wills will . . .'? I suppose that the meaning intended is roughly as follows: 'The customs surrounding marriage, and the extent to which children survived their parents, are revealed by the study of wills and are discussed in detail below.']

# AN EXERCISE IN HISTORICAL WRITING

## A medieval pilgrimage at Stanton, Suffolk

This is all the significant information known about a minor historical subject. It is given in the order in which it was accidentally found or positively looked for. Please absorb the detail with care, and then write your own piece of history. A specimen draft is provided on p. 81.

(1) British Museum, Lansdowne 64, MS 12826: Petition of Richard Sheparde, rector, to Lord High Treasurer, 1590: 'In tyme past the Church called Allsaintes had a Saint called St Parnell standinge in it, wherunto many resorted as Pilgrims & did offer, and therof great gayne was made, w$^{ch}$ in those daies much holpe the Minister of that Church, and now that lyvinge is much the lesser.'
*Note:* to understand this dedication, it might be worth consulting a Dictionary of Saints. The extract above was a chance discovery, based on a reference in W. A. Copinger, *Suffolk records and manuscripts,* V, 26; it immediately raised the question: where can I find more about this cult? Wills and ecclesiastical surveys were possible answers.

(2) *Nonarum inquisitiones* (1340/1), Record Commissioners, p. 72: 'Item de oblat' capell' Sce Petronille virg' vj$^s$ viij$^{d,}$.
(Translation: 'Item, in oblations to the chapel of St Petronilla the virgin, 6/8d')

(3) Suffolk Record Office (Bury St Edmunds), Will Register II ('Baldwyne'), f.135v: will of John Pyke of Stanton, 1451: 'Item lego ad ymag[in]is [sic] be' Petronill' iiij$^{d,}$.
(Translation: 'Item, I leave to the image of the Blessed Petronilla, 4d')

Ibidem, f.568v: will of Margaret Glover, widow, of Stanton, 1474: 'Item lego sum[m]o altar' ecc[les]ie sce' Petronille in villa de Stanton' predca' pro decimis & oblac[i]onibus meis oblit' iij$^s$ iiij$^{d,}$.
(Translation: 'Item, I leave to the high altar of the church of St Petronilla in the town of Stanton aforesaid, for my tithes and offerings forgotten, 3/4d')

(4) Suffolk Record Office (Ipswich), IC/AA2/1/196: will of Richard Spede, of Stanton, 1448: 'It[em] lego pro pict[ur]and' imag' bte marie exist' in capell' bte petronille iij$^s$ iiij$^d$'.
(Translation: 'Item, I leave for painting the image of the Blessed Mary in the chapel of the Blessed Petronilla, 3/4d')

(5) Suffolk Record Office (Bury St Edmunds), 574/14: memorandum that feoffees, named in charter attached, intended to provide two wax candles every Sunday for a year in All Saints church; one candle before the crucifix and one before the image of the Virgin. (14th century)

(6) *Letters & papers . . . of the reign of Henry VIII*, No. 364, p. 144: among the 'vain & fictitious relics' which Drs Layton and Legh noted at Bury Abbey, just before its dissolution in 1539, was the skull of St Petronilla, which 'simple people put on their heads hoping thereby to be delivered of fever'.

(7) Architectural evidence: All Saints church, Stanton, has three piscinae which reveal the positions of medieval altars – one in the chancel, one in the cramped north-east corner of the nave where the pulpit now stands, and the third in the spacious and stylish south aisle. The whole church appears to have been rebuilt *c.* 1300–20.

# A suggested draft

### The cult of St Petronilla at Stanton

All Saints' in Stanton is an ordinary parish church of no special architectural distinction. One is therefore surprised to learn that, for at least 200 years before the Reformation, it regularly attracted pilgrims. Richard Sheparde, a rector in Elizabethan times, revealed in a petition to the Lord High Treasurer that 'in tyme past the church called Allsaintes had a Saint called St Parnell [or Petronilla] standinge in it, wherunto many resorted as Pilgrims & did offer.'[1] So somewhere within this church was an image of that saint, possibly with a relic, which was revered not only in Stanton but further afield. In addition, we know that a special chapel was dedicated to St Petronilla from at least 1340, soon after All Saints was rebuilt in its present form, and that it contained an image of the Virgin Mary as well as one of St Petronilla herself.[2] To support the chapel and its images, visitors gave regular offerings and local residents left bequests in their wills. To Margaret Glover, a widow of Stanton who made her will in 1473, St Petronilla was so important that she named the whole church after her.[3]

But where, within the church, was St Petronilla's chapel? Three fourteenth-century piscinae betray the presence of medieval altars: one lies in the chancel, one in the cramped north-eastern corner of the nave, and the third in the south aisle. As the high altar was dedicated to All Saints and the nave altar could never have been within a chapel, we can presumably place St Petronilla's chapel at the east end of the spacious and stylish south aisle.

### References

1 B. M. Lansdowne 64, MSS 12826.
2 *Nonarum inquisitiones,* p. 72; also the will of Richard Spede of Stanton, 1448 (SRO(I): IC/AA2/1/196).
3 Will of John Pyke of Stanton, 1451 (SRO(B): Will Register II (Baldwyne), f.135v); will of Margaret Glover of Stanton, 1474 (ibidem, f.568v); memorandum for provision of wax candles, 14th century (SRO(B): 574/14).

81

# THE CHARACTERISTICS OF HISTORICAL LANGUAGE

The following is a tongue-in-cheek attempt to list words and phrases which seem commonplace in historical writing. In all seriousness one can neither recommend nor condemn this kind of language: it results from the historian's expression of complicated thoughts and judgements by a scrupulously careful choice of words – even at the risk of being thought fussy, pedantic and indecisive.

**Adverbs:** Perhaps... possibly... presumably... conceivably... arguably... apparently... admittedly... nearly... almost... partly...

**Adjectives:** Questionable... plausible... unproven... hypothetical... likely... reasonable... misleading...

**Negative expressions:** Not improbable... not a few... not infrequently...

**Conjunctions:** If... but... although... whereas... yet... nevertheless... notwithstanding... in spite of...

**Words of emphasis:** Furthermore... moreover... indeed... in fact... especially...

**Phrases:** It seems that... it may be... suggests (implies) that... one is tempted to say that... it is a reasonable assumption (hypothesis, interpretation) that... on balance, it would seem... the balance of opinion probably favours... the evidence so far as it goes... the meaning is not altogether clear... regrettably we are not told... fragmentary though the evidence is... there is no way of telling... caution forbids... it would be hazardous... our best evidence lies in... on the one/other hand...

**The language of reviews:** (Un)controlled imagination... (un)critical... (un)scholarly . . . respect for the truth . . . rooted in the evidence . . . ill-judged... axe to grind... politically prejudiced... heap of facts... shift of opinion... persuasive argument...

# STYLES OF HISTORICAL WRITING

All historical writing is in the last resort unique. Two people may use some of the same facts, but the total blend of information, the judgements and interpretations in which facts are embedded and the style by which an historical argument is expressed, can never be repeated a second time – even by the same writer.

Given that writing probably reveals more about a person's mind than any other activity, it is truly astonishing that so much careless and uncritical work is offered and published. This appendix gives short extracts from the work of five historians, which show the value of careful thought and style. After each extract, a few comments are given, in square brackets. Asterisks mark where references are given in the original.

(1) W. G. Hoskins, *The Midland peasant* (1957) pp. 278–9:

'The church was too closely linked with the masters in the nineteenth century: the wage-earners filled the chapels. Non-conformity had grown strong in Wigston all through the Georgian era. The return made to Parliament in 1829 revealed 520 Independents, 195 Wesleyan Methodists, 105 Primitive Methodists, and 30 General Baptists – a total of 850 nonconformists out of about 2100 inhabitants. In 1676 they had been about 4 per cent of the total population; by the 1720's about 16 per cent; and a hundred years later they were fully 40 per cent. Their strength had continued to increase in the mid-Victorian decades. The Wesleyans had put up a new chapel in 1839. Two years later the Independents had rebuilt and enlarged their attractive old Georgian meeting-place (first built in 1731), and in 1845 the Primitive Methodists blossomed forth in a new chapel. Here and there in odd corners behind the main streets, other little sects flourished obscurely, worshipping the Almighty in their own way in bare brick tabernacles as ugly as their own cottages. So in 1870 the empty Sunday streets would suddenly resound with the loud defiant singing of the chapels from one end of the village to the other, while from the parish church came the more subdued murmur of "the Conservative Party at prayer".'

[Hoskins' writing has an apparently easy elegance, which no doubt conceals a lot of hard work. The rise of nonconformity in Wigston Magna is convincingly demonstrated, first by the use of total figures and then by percentages. Throughout we are never in any doubt that figures mean people. Notice the value of imaginative phrases like 'flourished obscurely', 'loud defiant singing' and 'empty Sunday streets'. Characteristically too, this paragraph contains some of Hoskins' personal attitudes and prejudices, for example, his sympathy with the underdog and distrust of 'masters'.]

(2) David G. Hey, *An English rural community, Myddle under the Tudors and Stuarts* (1974), pp. 111 and 113:

'William Downton (1560–1629) was a "prudent" yeoman who rented extra land at Bilmarsh in addition to his father's land. He was succeeded by his son, Samuel, with whom the younger branch of the Downtons began its decline. Gough says he "was crooke backd, had a grim swarthy complection and long blacke haire. But hee was not so deformed in Body as debauched in behaviour . . . His prudent Father observing the idle and lewd courses of his son sought out a wife for him in time", and he married Elizabeth Botfield of Noneley, by whom he had two sons and five daughters. During her lifetime Samuel "lived in good fashion", but his wife died while the children were still young and, to the distress of his children, Samuel married his servant girl. The children all left home to go into service as soon as they could. Samuel quickly ran into debt and was forced to sell the lands he had gained by his first wife, but he could not sell his original tenement as it was bound by his first marriage settlement to his heirs. All he could do was to sell it for his life, and, hearing of this, his son, Thomas, borrowed money from his master and purchased the farm. Samuel left to sell ale in Cockshutt and for a time did well, but eventually fell into debt. He and his wife made a moonlight flit into Staffordshire, leaving their four children to be maintained by the parish. "Hee went a begging like an old decripite person and she carryed a box with pinnes . . . and laces. But after a while shee gott a new Sparke that travelled the Country and went away with him, and then this Samuel came again to Alderton to his son, Thomas, who maintained him during his Life."

'Thomas Downton, by his parsimony and hard work, recovered much of what had been lost. He managed to pay off all the money he had borrowed and built up a good stock of cattle. But then he unexpectedly married a woman who not only brought him nothing but took away all that he had. "Her name is Judith – shee was brought up all her lifetime as servant in some alehouse or other, and shee proved such a drunken woman as hath scarce beene heard of; shee spent her husband's estate soe fast that it seemed incredible . . . Her husband paid £10 at a time for alehouse scores." Thomas died in the closing years of the seventeenth century with his possessions almost gone, for he was forced to sell his farm, to Rowland Muckleston of Oswestry. What money he had left was spent by his wife within a couple of years of his death, and in 1701 she was living poorly in a little house in Myddle. She died a widow and pauper in 1735. The decline of the Downtons was complete.'

[Here is an absolutely clear, unpretentious style which seems just right for the simple but moving story being told – the decline of a once-prosperous yeoman family as a result of personal weakness and imprudent marriage over two generations. This is the kind of deeply personal, biographical history which the majority of local historians would like to write, because it seems at the very heart of local life. So far, admittedly, such writing has depended on the existence of exceptional sources like Gough's 'History of Myddle', Ralph Josselin's diary or detailed oral evidence. One wonders whether historical writing of this personal kind will ever come out of the new techniques of 'record linkage', on their own. Notice how David Hey resisted the temptation to overuse quotations, in spite of the attractions of Gough's colourful prose.]

(3) E. P. Thompson, *Whigs and hunters* (Peregrine, 1977), pp. 144–5:

'For a few months the Robin Hood of legend was incarnated in "King John".* The resentments of decades sheltered him and his band, as he rode openly about administering folk justice. His supporters seemed to be able to disappear as easily into the folds of popular concealment as did the Vietcong. Many of the incidents in north-east Hampshire . . . may very probably belong with the activities of this group, which may have been based near Farnham or Crondall.* Certainly the punishment of the zealous Sir John Cope by felling his young trees appears to fall in with the pattern of their actions. But if the Hampshire Blacks were in fact enrolled under oaths of fealty to "King John", very few would have been of the actual fraternity: the correspondent of the *London Journal* guessed at anything from thirty to a hundred, but only twenty or so were ever seen in action at one time. These well-disciplined rebels were however the precipitant of many other freelance actions, by poachers (and venison dealers), smugglers, fishermen, and foresters. All of these actions were, of course, seen by the authorities, within one common blur, as outrages by the Blacks. "King John", on at least one occasion, when smugglers smutted their faces and seized some wine, took pains to issue a disclaimer. The wine which they intercepted was on its way to the Prince of Wales, and the smugglers averred that they were delighted to have the means to make a loyal festival, and would be certain to drink the Prince's health. But "King John" put it out that henceforth to circumvent the Proclamation and to distinguish themselves from imitators the Blacks would disguise their faces in *white*.*'

[In this fascinating book on the woodland rebels of early Georgian England, Edward Thompson has adopted a more localised approach than he normally does as a social historian. Apart from a passing reference to the *London Journal,* this paragraph stands well back from the sources. It is a piece of narrative-cum-description, in which the author summarises a whole series of events in his own words. Thompson has a more complicated style than Hoskins or Hey: he uses longer words and has a penchant for abstract nouns like 'precipitant'. Occasionally the writing seems unnecessarily indirect, for example: 'Many of the incidents . . . may very probably belong with the activities of this group' or 'King John put it out that henceforth to circumvent the Proclamation . . .' The reference to the Vietcong seems apt, though it may date quickly.]

(4) Rowland Parker, *The common stream* (Paladin, 1976), p. 123:
   'What did those men do, then? Just this; between 1550 and 1620 they rebuilt the entire village. More than fifty houses were either erected on derelict sites or built to replace houses which were in a state of near collapse. Some were built in the old ramshackle way, or built entirely of old material re-used, and lasted no more than a hundred years or so. Most of them were built of new straight beams of oak, or of sound timbers salvaged from a previous house. They were built to last, and last they did, as witness the fact that in this one village alone twenty of them are standing at the present day. In this and neighbouring villages there are thousands of oak beams, mostly hidden by plaster on the outside, which were sawn from trees four hundred years ago, and amongst them are many which were sawn five or even six hundred years ago. They constitute a monument not so much to the material prosperity of an age as to the good sense and good taste of two or three generations of men, common men for the most part who believed in quality and durability. Did it ever occur to them, I wonder, that the beams which they were putting to such good use had come from trees which, in many cases, had sprung from acorns planted by man or by nature at about the time of the Norman Conquest? Did *they* plant any acorns? I do not think so, for if they had we would be reaping the harvest today, and the sad truth is that there is little harvest to reap. . . .'

[Rowland Parker's book, though only a parish history, has had great commercial success. It has been read by vastly more people than normally read local history, so its qualities are worth careful analysis and discussion. The style is friendly, chatty and full of questions; at times it shows a genuine literary quality, as in the passage about the oak timbers in local houses; nobody can doubt the compassionate interest in human beings. But historically the contents frequently leave us uneasy and dissatisfied. In particular, the lack of references gives rise to the fear that imagination has been allowed to roam far beyond the evidence, instead of remaining rooted in it.]

(5) J. D. Chambers, 'The Vale of Trent', *Economic History Review Supplements,* 3 (1957), p. 61:

'A corroboration of the harsh picture of early factory life is usually looked for by local historians in the numerous entries of burials at Robinson's mills in the parish of Linby – "starved and murdered – three or four a week sometimes being placed beneath the grass in the Church Yard". They are certainly there; one in 1799, two in 1800, eleven in 1801, two in 1802, ten in 1803 and sixteen more between 1805 and 1811, a total of forty-two in thirteen years: not 163 as is usually stated.* This may be evidence of brutality and under-feeding, but it is strange that the entries only begin fifteen years after the mills had come into existence. A similar series of entries occurs at Hawksley and Davison's mill at Arnold: twenty-seven in 1801; twelve in 1802; eight in 1803; twelve in 1804; four in 1805 – again, we are told, the result of overwork, neglect and over-crowding.* This was notoriously a period of famine and fever; in all the parishes concerned, and in Nottingham, the burials in 1801 were among the highest in the whole series; and Messrs Hawksley and Davison made their name at this time by buying corn wherever they could get it, having it ground by their own steam mill and offering it for sale at a price lower than cost at Week Day Cross at Nottingham.* Were they feeding the people of Nottingham and starving their apprentices at Arnold? Or were the apprentices at Arnold – and at Linby – victims of the epidemic of smallpox that was raging outside and prompting a Nottingham surgeon to undertake free vaccination to all comers? When the mothers of the children saw that the practice was successful on his own son, and the son of a friend, they flocked to his surgery on Beastmarket Hill and the "worthy gentleman, instead of making a charge, thanked them for their attendance".'

[This paragraph was written by a distinguished pioneer of local and regional history, whose work has not yet received the recognition it deserves. It is not particularly easy reading with its detail, its long sentences and rather personal style of punctuation, but it is a good example of the critical historian at work, probing his sources, questioning the work of other historians and arguing a case. Chambers really makes his detail count. For all the statistics, we are left in no doubt that he is talking about people. Historians often ask open questions in their writings, but the questions towards the end of this paragraph are rhetorical. By them Chambers shows, in an undogmatic way, where he thinks the truth probably lies.]

# SOME RULES RECOMMENDED FOR SETTING OUT REFERENCES

*Note:* some of the following rules are generally accepted; others are a matter of personal choice, or of the system adopted by a particular journal or publisher. *The really vital principle is consistency.*

(1) If you are dealing with a printed book, give the information in this order: name of the writer, with the initials or Christian name first; the title underlined (to a printer, this means the use of italics); the publisher and place of publication (which are optional); the year of publication, preferably in brackets to avoid confusion with page numbers. If you wish to quote a particular part of the book, indicate the page or pages thus: p. 93 *or* pp. 93–5.

EXAMPLE: W. G. Hoskins, *Local history in England,* Longmans, London (1959), pp. 167–73

(2) If a book has more than one volume, the number of the relevant volume should be in Roman numerals, after the date of publication. In addition, the abbreviations 'p.' or 'pp.' should be dropped.

EXAMPLE: *Guide to the contents of the Public Record Office,* HMSO, London (1968), III, 40

The same principle applies to journals with their multiple volumes. Their titles are often abbreviated.

EXAMPLE: *Agricultural History Review,* XV (1967), 18; or *Ag. H. R.,* XV (1967), 18

(3) When an article from a journal is being quoted, the title of the article should appear in inverted commas, and the title of the journal underlined (i.e. italicised).

EXAMPLE: E. A. Wrigley, 'Family limitation in pre-industrial England', *Economic History Review,* 2nd series, XIX (1966) 82–109.

(4) Reference to manuscript sources should be given as follows: some description of the source, with an indication of date; then, in brackets, the official reference and, if necessary, the number of the individual piece, page or folio.

EXAMPLE: Extent of the manor of Writtle, Essex, 1304 (PRO: C133/113(1)) (Note: the description and date need not be given, if already mentioned in the text.)

(5) Be consistent in your use of punctuation. To make the printed page less spotty, it makes sense to minimise the number of full-stops and capital letters (for example, PRO rather than P.R.O.; *The world we have lost* rather than *The World we have Lost*).

(6) Latin terms are commonplace in references, and have to be used accurately. For example:

   i Ibid. (for *ibidem*, Latin for 'at the same place'). This is used when a reference repeats the one immediately before. It should be underlined when the source is printed, and followed by a page number.

   ii Op. cit. (for *opere citato*, Latin for 'in the work quoted'). This refers to a work which has already been quoted, but not immediately before. The author's name is given first.

   EXAMPLE: W. G. Hoskins, *op. cit.*, p. 165

   This Latin phrase is sometimes used in a very irritating way, forcing the reader to look back through scores, even hundreds, of pages to find the original reference. In such cases, it would be far better to repeat the whole reference.

   iii Passim (Latin for 'in every part'). This indicates that the whole of a particular book or article is relevant. It follows a normal reference, and appears instead of a page number.

## Bibliographies

Substantial pieces of written history should also incorporate a bibliography. This is a complete list of all the sources which have been consulted, both printed and manuscript. Descriptions of individual works will have the same form as ordinary references, except that the author's surname should precede his initials or Christian name. Items should be listed in the following special order:

(1) Manuscripts (by custom, the British Library is given pride of place).

(2) Printed books and articles (primary sources should come before secondary).

# Historical dating

(The answers to the exercise on p. 53)

(1) 20th Nov., 1289–19th Nov. 1290
(2) 22nd June, 1385–21st June, 1386
(3) 29th May, 1660–29th Jan., 1661
(4) 2nd Nov.
(5) 9th Oct.
(6) 7th July

(7) 6th April, 1309
(8) 4th September, 1336
(9) 3rd March, 1418
(10) 4th September, 1363
(11) 9th Jan., 1710

---

'I say This only, Next to the immediate discharge of my Holy Office, I know not how in any course of studies I could have better served my Patron, my People and my Successors, than by preserving the Memoirs of this Parish and the adjacent Parts, which before lay remote from common notice, and in a few years had been buried in unsearchable Oblivion. If the present Age be too immersed in Cares and Pleasures, to take any Relish or to make any Use of these discoveries, I then appeal to Posterity: for I believe the times will come when Persons of better inclination will arise, who will be glad to find any Collection of this nature; and will be ready to supply the Defects, and carry on the Continuation of it.'

White Kennett, Vicar of Ambrosden in Oxfordshire, 1695
(*Parochial Antiquities . . . of Ambrosden, Burcester and other adjacent parts . . .* pp. v–vi)

'Good historians, I suspect, whether they think about it or not, have the future in their bones. Besides the question "Why?" the historian also asks the question "Whither?"'

E. H. Carr, *What is history?* (Pelican, 1964), p. 108

# INDEX

Accounts, 25
Adult education, 11, 19
Analysis:
  examples of, 54–6, 57, 58
  mathematical, 25–6
  methods of, 22–7
  *see also* Interpretation
Antiquaries, work of early, 22–3
Appendices, 43
Archaeology, 18, 28–9
Archives, 15
Articles, definite and indefinite, 41

Background knowledge, 16–17, 24
Batley, James, 43
Bibliographies:
  need for, 12
  style of, 89
Bloch, Marc, 34

*Calendars,* 49
Cambridge Group for the History of Population and Social Structure, 11, 57, 63
Carew, Richard, 6
Censuses, 27–8
Centre for East Anglian Studies, 17
Chambers, J. David, 6, 87
Chapels, 10
Charter Rolls, 49
Charters, 5, 22, 25
Cheney, C. R., 21, 53
'Chorography of Suffolk', 23
Church guides, 9–10
Clarke, Dennis, 67
'Cliometrics', 25–6
Close Rolls, 49
Cobbold, Richard, 29
Colvin, H. M., 30
Commercial directories, *see* Directories
Communities, study of groups of, 6

Council minutes, 26
County histories, 6, 13
Court rolls, 11, 25, 61
Creigh, Dorothy, 43

Dating, 21, 53, 90
Deaneries, 6
Dialect words, 20
Diplomatic, science of, 22
Directories, 26, 27
Documents:
  analysis of, 22–7
  details, systems of handling, 25–6
  indexes for, 25
  publication of, 12
  use of, 22–9
Domesday Book, 12, 49

Ecclesiastical Taxation (of 1291), 49
Editing, 15–16, 52
Editors, 2
Elton, Geoffrey, 2–3
'English topography', 3
Engravings, 18
Evidence, *see* Documents *and* Landscape

Fieldhouse, Roger, 59
Finberg, H. P. R., ix, 30, 36
Footnotes, 42, 43 *see also* References
Forgeries, 22

Garrard, Rachel, 58
Gelling, Margaret, 17
Gooder, Eileen, 20
Gough, Richard, 5, 6
Group work, 11

Hallam, H. E., 6
Halliwell, J. O., 20

Handwriting *see* Palaeography
Hearth-tax returns, 25, 31, 56
*Henry VIII, Letters and Papers of the reign of,* 49
Hexter, J. H., 10
Hey, David, 5, 8, 84–5
Historians:
  specialisation of, 9–10
  work of early, 22–3
  *see also* Local historians
Historical Association, 17, 19
Historical Manuscripts Commission, 49
History:
  language of, 82
  teaching of, 2–3
  *see also* Local history
*History,* 17
Hoskins, W. G., ix, 7–8, 14, 31, 33, 43, 63, 66, 83–4
'House repopulation', 28
Hundred Rolls, 49
Hundreds, 6
Hunnisett, R. F., 44, 52

Indexes, 12, 16, 25, 43–4 *see also under* Sources
*Inquisition of the Ninth* (of 1340/1), 49
Inquisitions Post Mortem, 49
Interpretation, 11, 16, 22, 27, 30, 35 *see also* Analysis

Jargon, 39–40
Jenkins, David, 8
Jennings, Bernard, 43

Kennedy, B. H., 20

Lambarde, William, 6
Landscape, 18, 28–9
Latin, 20, 52
Lay subsidies, 31, 54, 56, 61–2

*Local Historian, The,* 17, 43
Local historians:
  contacts between, 17
  motives of, 4–5
  range of, ix–x
  task of, 10
  *see also following entries*
Local history:
  educational development of, 1, 12
  human contact and, 17–18
  humaneness of, 4
  national organisation for, 1
  specialists and, 17
  state of, 1–3
  teaching of, 7
  *see also preceding entry*
Local history societies, 8
Local History, British Association for, 17
*Local Population Studies,* 11

McCulloch, Diarmaid, 22–3
Macfarlane, Alan, 11, 60–1
Manorial surveys, 5
Manuscripts, 15
Maps, 18, 28
Marshall, John, 34
Mathematical analysis, 25–6
*Miscellanies,* 49
Mullins, E. L. C., 49
Munby, Lionel, 36

Names, 28
Newman, Mrs, 9
Newspapers, 26
Newton, Robert, 26
*Notes and Queries,* 49
Note-taking, 14
Nouns, accumulations of, 40
Numeracy, 41 *see also* 'Cliometrics'

Oral evidence, 18
Owen, Dorothy, 14

Palaeography, 19, 20, 52
Palliser, D. M., 63
Parishes, significance of boundaries, 6
Parish histories, 8, 10, 67
Parish registers, 11, 25, 27, 57, 64
Parker, Roland, 86
Patent Rolls, 49
Photographs, 18
Poll-books, 25, 31
Poor-law records, 5
Prejudice, 37
Present, recording of, 8–9, 12
Privy Council, Acts of, 49
Probate inventories, 24, 25, 58
Public Record Office, 49
Publishers, 2, 43
Publishing, range of, 17
Pugh, R. B., ix

Quotations, 36–7

Rate-books, 25
Ravensdale, Jack, 6
Record Commissioners, 49
Record offices, 15, 19
Records, publication of, 12
Record societies, local, 49
References:
    balance in, 42
    checking, 42
    Harvard system, 43
    placing of, 43
    rules for, 88–9
    unread works, 43
    use of, 42
    see also Footnotes
Regional history, 6–7, 12, 25
Rentals, 25
Research:
    defects in, 1
    organisation of, 14–15
    storage of results, 14–15
    writing and, 1, 32
    see also Subjects, choosing

Reviews, 17
Rogers, Alan, ix, 6, 35
Roget's Thesaurus, 41
Rowe, D. J., 9

Secondary sources, 16, 18
Sources:
    assessment of, 60–2
    examples of important, 49–50
    indexes of original, 50
    notes on, 15
    plenitude of, 8
    printed, 15–16, 49–50
    relating varied, 27–9, 59, 60, 61
    search for, 14–18
    storage of information from, 14–15
    see also previous entry and Documents
Spufford, Margaret, 6, 9, 11, 16, 61–2
Stapleton, Barry, 11
Stephens, W. B., ix, 14
Storage of information, 14–15
Stoyel, Anthony, 67
Style, 38–9, 40–1, 71–5, 83–7
Subjects, choosing:
    factors influencing, 4, 5
    place and, 5–7
    sources and, 4
    themes, 9–11
    time span, 7–9

Thompson, E. P., 37, 85–6
Tithe awards, 27, 28
'Total history', 10–11
Town histories, 8, 10
Townscape, 18
'Trails', 10
Transcriptions, 11, 12:
    control of paper, 20–1
    defects of, 15–16
    finding, 49
    methods, 19–20
    mistakes made, 19
    rules for, 51–2
Translations, 12, 52:

difficulties of, 20
  finding, 49
Trinder, Barrie, 29
'Tunnel history', 10
Turner, Michael, 17

Verbs, devaluing of, 40–1
Victoria County History, 14–15, 49
Voters' lists, 26

Wapentakes, 6
Willan, T. S., 60
Williams, Glanmore, 9
Wills, 11, 25
Words:
  choice of, 41
  order of, 41
  technical, 39–40
Workhouses, 16
Worth, R. H., 30
Wright, Joseph, 20

Wrigley, E. A., 27
Writing:
  argument, ordering of, 31, 63
  chronology and, 36
  comparisons in, 31
  examples analysed, 63–70, 71–5, 76–8, 83–7
  exercises in, 79–81
  final draft, 37–42
  first draft, 32, 81
  guidance, need for, ix
  guidelines for, 34–7
  prejudices and, 37
  preliminary notes for, 32
  readership, consideration of, 32–3
  rewriting, 38
  selectivity, 35, 36
  structure of, 30, 63
  timing of, 30
  see also Jargon, Quotations, References, Style, Subjects, choosing, Words and under Research